ANTONY SHER

Antony Sher is an   frica,
he settled in England in 1968. ... ...   vels –
Middlepost, The Indoor Boy, Cheap Lives, The Feast – and two
theatre journals – *Year of the King* and *Woza Shakespeare!*
(co-written with his partner Greg Doran). He has also published
a book of his paintings and drawings, *Characters*, and his
autobiography, *Beside Myself.*

As an Associate Artist of the Royal Shakespeare Company
he has played Richard III, Macbeth, Leontes, Shylock,
Tamburlaine the Great and Cyrano de Bergerac, as well as
Caesar in Massinger's *The Roman Actor*, Henry Carr in
Stoppard's *Travesties*, Johnnie in Fugard's *Hello and Goodbye*
and the title roles in John Marston's *The Malcontent* and Peter
Flannery's *Singer*.

At the Royal National Theatre he played the title roles in Pam
Gems' *Stanley* (also at the Circle in the Square Theatre, New
York), Brecht's *Arturo Ui* and Shakespeare's *Titus Andronicus*
(a co-production with the Market Theatre, Johannesburg).

Other theatre includes Harvey Fierstein's *Torch Song Trilogy*,
Mike Leigh's *Goosepimples* and Ronald Harwood's *Mahler's
Conversion.* Film and television credits include *Mrs Brown,
Alive and Kicking, The History Man* and *Macbeth.*

Among numerous awards he has won the Olivier Best Actor
Award on two occasions (*Stanley* and *Richard III/Torch Song
Trilogy*), the Evening Standard Best Actor Award (*Richard III*)
and the Peter Sellers Evening Standard Film Award (*Mrs Brown*).
The Universities of Liverpool and Exeter have both presented
him with an honorary Doctorate of Letters. In 2000 he was
knighted for his services to acting and writing.

In the same series

Caryl Churchill
BLUE HEART
CHURCHILL PLAYS: THREE
CHURCHILL: SHORTS
CLOUD NINE
FAR AWAY
HOTEL
ICECREAM
LIGHT SHINING IN
  BUCKINGHAMSHIRE
MAD FOREST
A NUMBER
THE SKRIKER
THIS IS A CHAIR
TRAPS

Ariel Dorfman
DEATH AND THE MAIDEN
READER
THE RESISTANCE TRILOGY
WIDOWS

David Edgar
ALBERT SPEER
DR JEKYLL AND MR HYDE
EDGAR:SHORTS
PENTECOST
THE PRISONER'S DILEMMA
THE SHAPE OF THE TABLE

Helen Edmundson
ANNA KARENINA
THE CLEARING
THE MILL ON THE FLOSS
MOTHER TERESA IS DEAD
WAR AND PEACE

Kevin Elyot
THE DAY I STOOD STILL
MOUTH TO MOUTH
MY NIGHT WITH REG

Peter Flannery
SINGER

Pam Gems
DEBORAH'S DAUGHTER
STANLEY

Stephen Jeffreys
THE CLINK
A GOING CONCERN
I JUST STOPPED BY TO SEE
  THE MAN
THE LIBERTINE

Tony Kushner
ANGELS IN AMERICA
HOMEBODY/KABUL

Mike Leigh
ECSTASY
SMELLING A RAT

Conor McPherson
DUBLIN CAROL
McPHERSON: FOUR PLAYS
PORT AUTHORITY
THE WEIR

Gary Mitchell
AS THE BEAST SLEEPS
THE FORCE OF CHANGE
TEARING THE LOOM
  & IN A LITTLE WORLD
  OF OUR OWN
TRUST

Presnyakov Brothers
PLAYING THE VICTIM
TERRORISM

Vassily Sigarev
BLACK MILK
PLASTICINE

Joshua Sobol/David Lan
GHETTO

Sophie Treadwell
MACHINAL

Steve Waters
WORLD MUSIC

Nicholas Wright
CRESSIDA
MRS KLEIN
VINCENT IN BRIXTON
WRIGHT: FIVE PLAYS

Antony Sher

I.D.

inspired by the book
A Mouthful of Glass
by Henk van Woerden

NICK HERN BOOKS
London
www.nickhernbooks.co.uk

A Nick Hern Book

I.D. first published in Great Britain in 2003 as a paperback original
by Nick Hern Books Limited, 14 Larden Road, London W3 7ST

I.D. copyright ©2003 by Antony Sher

Antony Sher has asserted his right to be identified as
the author of this work

Typeset by Country Setting, Kingsdown, Kent CT 14 8ES
Printed and bound in Great Britain by Bookmarque, Croydon, Surrey

ISBN 1 85459 754 X

A CIP catalogue record for this book is available from
the British Library

CAUTION   All rights whatsoever in this play are strictly reserved.
Requests to reproduce the text in whole or in part should be
addressed to the publisher.

Amateur Performing Rights Applications for performance,
including readings and excerpts, by amateurs should be addressed
to the Performing Rights Manager, Nick Hern Books, 14 Larden
Road, London W3 7ST, *fax* +44 (020) 8735 0250, *e-mail*
info@nickhernbooks.demon.co.uk, except as follows:

Australia Dominie Drama, 8 Cross Street, Brookvale 2100,
fax (2) 9905 5209, *e-mail* dominie@dominie.com.au

New Zealand: Play Bureau, PO Box 420, New Plymouth,
fax (6) 753 2150, *e-mail* play.bureau.nz@xtra.co.nz

United States of America and Canada: The Mic Cheetham
Literary Agency, 11-12 Dover Street, London W1S 4LJ ,
fax +44 (0) 20 7495 5777, *e-mail* mic@miccheetham.com

Professional Performing Rights Applications for performance by
professionals in any medium and in any language throughout the
world should be addressed to the Mic Cheetham Literary Agency,
11-12 Dover Street, London W1S 4LJ , *fax* +44 (0) 20 7495 5777,
e-mail mic@miccheetham.com

No performance of any kind may be given unless a licence has
been obtained. Applications should be made before rehearsals
begin. Publication of this play does not necessarily indicate its
availability for performance.

FOR NANCY MECKLER

with my thanks

S.A. BURGER — S.A. CITIZEN

0 2 2 1 0 7 9 7 1

BLANKE — WHITE PERSON
PERSOONSKAART
IDENTITY CARD

MANLIK – MALE

SHER A

PRETORIA 1.2.65   Sekretaris van Binnelandse Sake
Secretary for the Interior

REPUBLIEK VAN SUID-AFRIKA—REPUBLIC OF SOUTH AFRICA

Author's Note

I was in my last year of high school in Cape Town when, on Tuesday 6th September 1966, the Prime Minister Hendrik Verwoerd was assassinated. The event was intensely dramatic in every sense. The man known as the Architect of Apartheid had been stabbed to death inside parliament itself. The assassin was a temporary parliamentary messenger – Demetrios Tsafendas, who claimed he'd been driven to do the deed by a giant tapeworm that lived inside of him. He was declared mad, unfit to stand trial, and vanished from sight. But the strangeness and anarchy of the event made a huge impact on me; briefly upturning everything that seemed so solid and indestructible about the South Africa of my youth.

In 2000 I heard that the Dutch author Henk van Woerden had written a biography of Tsafendas, *A Mouthful of Glass.* The book had barely hit the shelves of my local Waterstone's before I'd bought a copy, read it in one gulp and was on a plane to Amsterdam to meet with van Woerden. I felt there was a play in this story. Would he let me acquire the stage rights?

It was only after he agreed that I realised I didn't actually know how to do it. Quite apart from the fact that I'd never attempted a play before, it seemed to me that van Woerden's book, although beautifully and movingly written, was only about Tsafendas, and for it to work as a drama, it needed the other half of the story: Verwoerd. The two men were obsessed by the same thing – identity – though in very different ways: Tsafendas in a personal sense; Verwoerd on a national scale. Yet the last thing I wanted to write was a history lesson. Maybe an answer lay in the giant tapeworm – maybe here was another character? Ideas were growing in my mind. But how to transform them into a piece of theatre?

I had two strokes of luck. I took the project to Sue Higginson at the National Theatre Studio and she offered to help develop it. Next, the director Nancy Meckler came on board. Her guidance proved to be invaluable over the two years that followed, with a series of workshops and readings at the Studio, and successive drafts of the script. Several members of the present cast attended the workshops and readings and also made important contributions. As did those people who were invited along to talk to us: three distinguished South African journalists – Stanley Uys (who'd actually witnessed the assassination from the reporter's gallery in parliament that day), Anthony Sampson and Sylvester Stein – and psychologist Morris Nitsun.

Although *A Mouthful of Glass* was the original inspiration for the play, I found another book very useful – *Verwoerd is Dead* by Jan Botha – and two documentary films quite indispensable: Guy Spiller's *The Liberal and the Pirate* and especially Lisa Key's *Furiosus*. Liza Key also allowed me to view the rushes of her film, with extensive footage of her visits to Tsafendas during his last years.

When Nancy and I finally felt we had a working script we asked Mike Attenborough to read it. He responded positively and offered to schedule it into his first season as the new Artistic Director of the Almeida. I am immensely grateful for that typically Attenborough-ish show of commitment and enthusiasm.

By chance, I found my old South African I.D card the other day. It's dated 1965, just a year before Tsafendas walked over to Verwoerd on the floor of the House and drew out a dagger. As I stare at the face on the card – quite apart from a feeling of disbelief that I ever looked so innocent – I am reminded again of how the assassination impacted on the boy called Sher A. Thirty-seven years later that boy, now deep inside me, is watching goggle-eyed again as we prepare to retell this story as a play.

Antony Sher
London, July 2003.

Principal Characters

DEMETRIOS TSAFENDAS, *a drifter*
HENDRIK VERWOERD, *the Prime Minister*
BETSIE VERWOERD, *his wife*
LINTWURM, *a parasite*
JOHN VORSTER, *various Cabinet posts, later Prime Minister*
HELEN DANIELS, *a Cape Coloured spinster*
GAVRONSKY,*Chief Government Psychiatrist*

SIPHO, *a black nurse (the same actor also playing Farm
   Labourer, Tramp, Streetsweeper, 3 Death Row Prisoners)*
FATHER DANIELS, *a Cape Coloured lay preacher*
GOMES, *a Portuguese doctor*
KRIEL, *a Reclassification Official*
PRATT, *a wealthy farmer*
CLOETE, *a Visa Official, SA House, London*
CITY GENT, *SA House, London*
SCHALK, *Senior Parliamentary Messenger*
MANOLIS, *Greek bosun on the Eleni*
NIKKI, *Greek cook on the Eleni*
DAISY, *a Cape Coloured prostitute*
MULLER, *a harbour policeman*
MINISTER, *Ministry of the Interior*
JUNIOR CLERK, *Ministry of the Interior*
BUYTENDAG, *personal bodyguard to Verwoerd*
FRANK WARING, *Sports Minister*
DR FISHER, *an MP*
MR JUSTICE PIENAAR, *a high-ranking judge*

Secondary Characters

INMATES 1, 2
MESSENGERS 1, 2, 3, 4
PUPILS 1,2

Non-Speaking Characters

Asylum Inmates, Asylum Orderlies, The Christian Church
Congregation, Rand Show Dignitaries, Rand Show Bodyguard,
Visa Applicants in SA House, Trafalgar Square Demonstrators,
Stepmother Marika, Displaced People, Customs Officials,
Policemen, Death Row Warders, Followers of Betsie Verwoerd

The Action

takes place mostly in South Africa between 1960 and 1999, with a few sequences earlier and elsewhere.

The Set

needs to be a very adaptable space, allowing many locations to be created quickly and simply.

The Cast

(of about twelve) need to play a host of different roles with the minimum of disguise

Scenes

ACT ONE

1   Sterkfontein Psychiatric Hospital, Krugersdorp, 1999.
2   The Daniels' home, Cape Town, 1965.
3   Verwoerd's private room, 1965.
4   The Daniels' home, Cape Town, 1965.
5   Dr Gomes' consulting room, Lourenco Marques, 1935.
6   Reclassification Office, Cape Town, 1965.
7   Travels round the world, 1942-1960.
8   Rand Show, Milner Park, Joburg, 1960.
9   Hospital room, South Africa, 1960.
10   South Africa House, Trafalgar Square, London, 1960.
11   Prime Minister's Office, South Africa, 1960.
12   Wasteland.
13   Oranje Asylum, Bloemfontein, 1961.
14   The Botanical Gardens, Cape Town, 1966.
15   The House of Assembly, Cape Town, 1966.

ACT TWO

16   Messengers' corridor, Parliament, Thurs 1 Sept 1966.
17   'Eleni' gangplank, Docks, Thurs night/Fri morn.
18   Messengers' corridor, Parliament, Fri 2 Sept 1966.
19   Tsafendas' room, Sat, Sun, Mon, 3, 4, 5 Sept 1966.
20   Various places, mainly Parliament, Tues 6 Sept 1966.
21   Dr Gavronsky's consulting room, Tues 6 Sept 1966.
22   State Funeral,1966.
23   Prime Mininster's Office, 1966.
24   Death Row, Pretoria Maximum Security, 1966-1994.
25   Sterkfontein Psychiatric Hospital, Krugersdorp,
       1994-1999.

I.D. was first presented at the Almeida theatre, London, on
4 Septemner 2003, with the following cast:

GAVRONSKY / BUYTENDAG / GOMES	Jon Cartwright
PRATT / MULLER / DR FISHER	Jonathan Duff
LINTWURM	Alex Ferns
JOHN VORSTER / KRIEL	Paul Herzberg
FATHER DANIELS / MANOLIS	Peter Landi
SIPHO	Lucian Msamati
CITY GENT / SCHALK / NIKKI / JUNIOR CLERK	
	Oscar Pearce
DEMETRIOS TSAFENDAS	Antony Sher
HELEN DANIELS / DAISY	Cleo Sylvestre
FRANK WARING / JUDGE PIENAAR	Christopher Wells
HENDRIK VERWOERD	Marius Weyers
BETSIE VERWOERD	Jennifer Woodburne

Other parts played by members of the Company.

Direction Nancy Meckler
Design Katrina Lindsay
Lighting Johanna Town
Music Ilona Sekacz
Movement Scarlett Mackmin
Sound John Leonard
South Africa Music Consultant Sello Maake ka Ncube

ACT ONE

Scene 1

In the darkness, we hear a voice:

TSAFENDAS. I dream of a girl . . . waiting for me . . . somewhere in Africa . . .

> *Lights reveal Sterkfontein Psychiatric Hospital, 1999. The inmates are a listless, heavily sedated group, all wearing regulation dressing-gowns: white with coloured stripes. Old* TSAFENDAS *(aged eighty-one) is sitting in a big bath chair. A black male nurse –* SIPHO *– is patiently trying to feed him from a bowl of soft food. Rather deaf,* TSAFENDAS *speaks to* SIPHO *in loud little bursts.*

TSAFENDAS. . . . It feels true. I think I'll find her. Read the old stories. It turns out alright, okeydokee. He gets there. The hero. He sails round the world . . . but gets there in the end. And hey presto. There she is . . . waiting for him . . .

SIPHO. OK, and open for me –

TSAFENDAS. Wha'?

> SIPHO *manages to feed a spoonful.* TSAFENDAS *eats contentedly.*

TSAFENDAS (*sings*). 'When you're smiling, when you're smiling, the whole world smiles with you.' Always been my motto. Others are worse off, clouds have silver linings. (*Examines his own hands closely.*) See these spots. My father had spots like these. I'm him now. Just falling through the years, to and fro. You spend ages trying to work out who you are. And in the end it's not you. It's him.

SIPHO. Mm-hh. I think my mother's in me sometimes. I think it's maybe why I do this job, heh. My mother . . .

TSAFENDAS (*vaguely*). My mother? No, no . . .

SIPHO. What?

TSAFENDAS. . . . My mother. Where?

Examines his hands again. SIPHO *shrugs, tries another spoonful.* TSAFENDAS *rubs his stomach.*

SIPHO. What? Is it heartburn?

TSAFENDAS. Wha'?

SIPHO (*loudly into his ear*). Heartburn – is it?

TSAFENDAS. Is it? I had a worm once.

SIPHO *hesitates – this is a big subject – and waits.* TSAFENDAS *is still.*

SIPHO. Go on. It's OK. You're OK now, no more trouble. Talk.

TSAFENDAS (*smiles shrewdly*). Talk, talk, talk. Questions and answers. All my life . . . 'Daisy, Daisy, give me your answer true . . . ' Who are you, what are you, where are you going? Oh, you can duck and dodge a bit, y'know. But when it comes to the big question – the big why – this calls for the truth, and nothing but. Why did you do it? Well, it was because of this. I dreamed of a girl . . . waiting for me . . . somewhere in Africa.

SIPHO *shrugs affectionately, wipes* TSAFENDAS' *mouth and exits.* TSAFENDAS *rubs his stomach again. The sensation grows, becoming more and more painful. He writhes. Another figure is slowly born from his belly.* LINTWURM. *A smiling, seedy bar-fly type, speaking in a smoky South African drawl. He's wearing goggles – which he pushes onto his forehead:*

LINTWURM (*to audience*). Assassination. A word you can taste hey? As-sas-si-nation. A tasty word for a tasty deed. Ass-as-sin-ation. Hear the ass in there and also the sin. Ass-a-sin-nation. Who is the ass, who does the sin, and what about the nation? Asssasssinashhhhhhhh . . .

LINTWURM *gives way to* TSAFENDAS *who rises, sheds his dressing gown, and picks up two large old suitcases . . .*

Scene 2

LINTWURM. . . . We're falling through the years folks . . .
  ten, twenty, thirty years . . . it's 1965 now . . . and
  Demetrios has turned up in that sunny, stormy ol' place
  called the Cape of Good Hope . . .

  *The sound of seagulls circling overhead. Lights up on a
  room with a single bed. TSAFENDAS (aged 47) enters,
  puts down the cases, and waits. LINTWURM watches from
  the sidelines. HELEN DANIELS enters – a Cape Coloured
  spinster, plump and bespectcled – carrying a cup of tea and
  plate of Marie biscuits. TSAFENDAS speaks and hears
  normally now; his accent is Southern African. He's tubby,
  gentle-spirited, optimistic – yet there's a clumsiness too, a
  battered quality: a man who's lived rough most of his life.*

TSAFENDAS. Oh how kind.

HELEN. Here you are now.

TSAFENDAS. Thank you, Miss Daniels . . . (*Starts scoffing
  the biscuits and slurping at the tea.*) . . . Dankie, obrigada
  menina.

  She makes to go.

TSAFENDAS. Bitte, Fraulein – when's the first meeting?

HELEN. Agh no, not till tomorrow arvie. The people, they
  usually start turning up after work. So usually we can get
  going roundabout five-thirty, six.

TSAFENDAS. Can't wait, cannot wait! 'All things bright and
  beautiful . . . ' (*Opening the cases.*) End of a long journey,
  Miss Daniels, a loooonnnggg journey.

HELEN. Is Durban really mos' that far?

TSAFENDAS. Before Durban, Miss Daniels.

HELEN. And where was you then?

TSAFENDAS. Lourenco. Before then – Lisbon, Beirut, East
  Jerusalem, Hamburg, London, Brussels, Paris, Piraeus, Ellis
  Island . . . must I go on?

HELEN. Haai, and I thought you were just from the Cuban Hat Tearoom, Durban.

TSAFENDAS. No, no, the seven seas, Miss Daniels, the seven seas.

She starts to leave again.

HELEN. The bath tin's in the yard, the lav's down the end. I'll get you a towel . . .

TSAFENDAS. Ah, min kanete ton kopo despinis! (*Produces a worn grey towel from one case.*) . . . Sheets and blankets too.

HELEN. Oh but I made the bed up . . .

TSAFENDAS. Oh . . .

HELEN. . . . Our sheets are clean.

TSAFENDAS. Of course they are, 'course, thank you.

HELEN. You should sleep well tonight anyhow. After all that travelling.

Pause. She gestures to the cases.

HELEN. If there's anything that needs washing . . . ?

TSAFENDAS. Ah, parakalo, efcharisto, parakalo!

Sniffing at items, he separates clean and dirty clothes.

HELEN. Ja you mos' told me . . . thanks for the letters by the by . . .

TSAFENDAS. No, and for yours.

HELEN. . . . Told me that you speak . . . how many tongues is it?

TSAFENDAS. Oh five, six, but first and foremost I am a Professor of English. (*Emphatically.*) English as a foreign language!

HELEN. Is English a foreign language?

TSAFENDAS. It is in Istanbul. (*Proudly produces a book from one case.*) 'Ogretmen Not Defteri – property of Tarhaban College, Istanbul'. Or Constantinople as we sometimes say in the Orient, salam alaikem, alahu akbar.

He starts unpacking: a hammer, a saw, a file.

HELEN. My glory. You need these to teach English?

TSAFENDAS (*laughing*). No, no, when I teach English, I need these . . .

More books.

HELEN. 'The Concise Oxford Dictionary' . . . 'Poems Old And New' . . .

TSAFENDAS. I wandered lonely as a cloud . . . (*Popping on a builder's hard-hat.*) And then sometimes I bend to honest toil . . . (*Exchanging it for a sailor's cap.*) . . . Or sail the ocean wave . . .

HELEN (*laughing shyly*). Hey, look at you now!

TSAFENDAS. But man must also rest . . .

He shows swimming trunks.

HELEN (*blushing*). Haai!

TSAFENDAS. And he must eat.

He shows saucepans.

HELEN. Agh siss, man – all mixed up with the swim broeks!

TSAFENDAS. And – and – and . . .

As he unpacks more items, a small brown photograph falls out. He shows it to her, handling it with tenderness.

TSAFENDAS. My granny, my yia-yia, yia yiaka mou. She brought me up when I was little. Greek – but living in Alexandria. Used to tell me a story. The greatest story ever told, she said, greater even than the Bible . . .

HELEN. Haai, shame on you.

TSAFENDAS. No, no, listen . . . 'Andhra moi ennepe Musa, polytropon, Hos mala pola plahthi' . . . this is how it begins . . . 'The Man o Muse, tell about the Man, the Man of many whiles' . . . the Wanderer, who endured incredible travels and travails, but always remained determined to find his way home. Where the lovely Penelope sits waiting for him.

Weaving at her loom, weaving and unweaving. She'll wait as long as it takes. She'll wait till he gets home. (*Beams at her.*) . . . Penelope.

HELEN. Penelope . . . ?

TSAFENDAS: Yes his wife . . . yes . . . (*Becomes embarrassed – points to the empty biscuit plate.*) I say, could I have some more, please?

HELEN. Uhm, ja OK.

TSAFENDAS. Or a sandwich or even some polony if you've . . .

HELEN. Ja, we have.

She exits. TSAFENDAS *immediately glances over to* LINTWURM.

TSAFENDAS. How am I – ?

LINTWURM. Doing fine buddy, doing great.

TSAFENDAS. Bit nervous.

LINTWURM. Sure.

He gives TSAFENDAS *a reassuring hug. They slowly entwine – as they will occasionally during the play – twisting together like insects – becoming one organism.*

TSAFENDAS. Just think. All these years . . . well, my whole life really . . . and all the time she's been here, waiting for me, the girl of my dreams . . . (*Overcome with joy.*) It's incredible. And she's everything I ever . . . ! She is so beautiful!

LINTWURM *registers surprise.*

TSAFENDAS. Her spirit.

LINTWURM. Her spirit. Oh, OK – fuck me, for a moment there I thought we were talking tits 'n poes.

TSAFENDAS. Tsk! Shh.

LINTWURM. Thought we were talking her thick kleurling gob locked round your neglected ol' knob.

TSAFENDAS (*covering his ears*). Shush – shush!

He quickly recovers as HELEN *enters with slices of polony on a plate.*

TSAFENDAS. Ah so kind, dankie, dankie . . . (*He wolfs the polony.*) Dankie for, y'know, everything. Can't tell you how nice it was when you wrote, 'There'll always be a bed for you here'.

HELEN. Always a bed for all brethren in the Daniels family home.

TSAFENDAS. How long for?

HELEN. Till you find your feet.

TSAFENDAS (*points down*). Found them!

She laughs bashfully. He eats more. Now music is heard – perhaps from a neighbour's radio – a sweet sixties melody. They look round, puzzled.

HELEN (*indicating the suitcases*). Is that from in there too?

TSAFENDAS *genuinely doesn't know. The music is tinny but magical.*

TSFENDAS (*mouth full*). May I – ?

They dance awkwardly. Then HELEN *becomes self-conscious, and exits. A shrill bell starts ringing in the distance.* LINTWURM *moves forward, doing a few dance steps of his own.*

LINTWURM (*to audience*). Like the tango, it takes two. It takes two to, hey? To do the deed and to be done unto. This takes two. Later on others may get named, get blamed . . . OK, hands up, I did it! (*Grins.*) . . . But for now let's say ass-a-sin-nation is like like a tango – or a fuck – and you gotta start with just two. Two people – and not just their pages in the history books. Now one of these two – (*Indicates* TSAFENDAS.) – he didn't even know he was gonna get into those books, while the other one, fuck me if he wasn't writing them himself. Ladies and gents, dames en here, boys and girls, I give you the guy they called The Granite Man of – The Grand Wizard of – The Architect of – Apartheid! The Right Honourable Doctor Hendrik Frensch Verwoooooerd . . . !

Scene 3

Tight spot on VERWOERD. *A slight smile always on his broad
face with its snout-like nose. His manner is very calm, very
civil, very persuasive. He manages to be both benign and
sinister.*

VERWOERD. . . . I saw Hitler speak once. This was in Berlin
in the twenties whilst I was engaged in post-graduate
studies. My inclination towards a German victory in the
'39 war is much documented and much misunderstood –
more a vote against Britain than anything else. Germany's
subsequent defeat can be explained in many ways,
including, I would argue, that they had a leader who simply
wasn't very good at public speaking. That oratorial style of
his – oh no, no – for me it simply got in the way of what he
was saying, though perhaps this was the point. For me it
was all just rather exaggerated and hysterical and fuelled by
quite the wrong thing. Emotion. Hatred. There is no place
for hatred in the job of Leader. It is not about hatred of
others. It is about love of your own people. And this is, my
friends, at the very heart of the policy which I have sought
to refine in this country, the policy which has been so often
misrepresented, the policy which is called by the Afrikaans
word 'apartheid', but which could as easily and perhaps
much better be called a policy of 'good neighbourliness'.
I may not like who my neighbour is or what he believes in.
He might in fact represent everything I abhor and disavow.
But as long as he restricts himself to his property, and me
to mine, we need never come to blows, we need never be
tainted by one another's otherness. This does not mean we
can't pop across to borrow a cup of sugar, or say a polite
how d'you do, but on a profound level we must remain
apart from one another, sealed off, immune, pure. (*Slight
pause.*) I have always regarded myself very fortunate in my
training as a young man. First at Stellenbosch University,
and then abroad, at the Universities of Leipzig, Hamburg,
and indeed Berlin, where one winter's evening, in a
crowded beer hall, I had the rather unmemorable experience
of hearing The Great Orator orate. My training was, as

some might know, in the subject of Psychology. This
enabled me, as I moved from the sunlit fields of academia
to the somewhat rougher arena of political combat, to find
ways of communicating my message that are always
civilised and tranquil. You don't have to wave your hands
around and screech at the top of your voice. You can
employ other methods. Now yes, some might find these
methods less arresting, less theatrical certainly, but let me
assure you I can make my points as effectively as Meneer
Adolf Hitler. I prefer what I call the Deadly Calm
Approach. Deadly Calm Approach. Deadly Calm. (*Slight
pause.*) Now what I was demonstrating there is the use of
Repetition. And the use of Emphasis. Repetition equals
Emphasis. This is vitally important. Are they hearing what
I say? Are they absorbing my message? I will go to any
lengths to ensure that my audience absorb my message.
I will deliberately modulate my tones – like this – speaking
quite softly, quite slowly – almost like a parent might use to
lull the little ones into slumber – and I can keep this up – as
I'm doing now – for a very, very long time – an hour or so,
say – which is actually neglible during some of my longer
orations. Now what would you expect the effect to be on
my audience? Yes, correct, absolutely correct – the eyelids
start to droop, the head to tilt downwards. But it is at this
point, this point exactly, that the method becomes most
effective. Which of us haven't started to drop off at the
wrong moment? At our child's school concert perhaps.
Or behind the wheel of a car, say. Think of the panic that
grips you. That dual pull. Of sleep and of responsibility.
Both such powerful forces. And there you are torn between
the two. Not unlike some unfortunate soul on that medieval
instrument, the rack. Now it is in this very state, I believe,
that my Cabinet hears me most clearly. And my Back-
benchers. And the Opposition, if there was one in this
country. My voice is echoing in their skulls, twice over,
three times, they are repeating my words to themselves, all
in this titanic battle to concentrate – for they know I *will*
cross-question them later – and now they are most inclined
to agree with absolutely everything I say. But please my
friends, please don't fool yourselves into believing this is

mere technique, a hypnotist's skill. No, no, no. The Deadly
Calm Approach only works if there is content to the orator's
words. It would not have worked for Mister Hitler. Most
crucially, it will only work if you know your facts. If-you-
know-your-facts. And believe me, I know my facts better
than any of my colleagues, I know their portfolios better
than they do, I know their ministries better than all of their
top advisors and experts put together. How do I achieve this?
Through work. I am prepared to work every hour God grants
me in this lifetime. I don't need to sleep. I don't need to eat.
I have been put on this sweet earth with a purpose, a gift
from on high. It is called Duty. And the Duty is to lead my
people, die Volk. And nothing – nothing – will make me
shirk my Duty. (*Slight pause.*) Which brings me to my
second point -

*He is suddenly interrupted by knocking. He sighs. The
knocking persists. The lights gradually reveal that he's in a
small private dressing room – with a full-length mirror on a
stand.*

BETSIE (*off*). Hendrik . . . why are you in there . . . talking?

VERWOERD. Practising, darling, just practising.

BETSIE (*off*). A speech?

VERWOERD. Hmn? Yes.

BETSIE (*off*). What about?

VERWOERD. Not sure yet.

BETSIE (*off*). But how can you practise a speech before you
know what it's about?

VERWOERD. Well, it just takes a few years in politics, my
darling.

BETSIE (*off*). Can I come in?

He quickly hides an open jar with fork sticking out.

VERWOERD. Yes.

BETSIE *enters. A small Afrikaner woman with darkish skin
and flat nose. She's wearing a nightdress and curlers.*

BETSIE. I woke up . . . you weren't there . . . and I suddenly
wanted to tell you something. Just how very much I love you.

VERWOERD. Oh . . . (*He embraces her with real feeling.*)

BETSIE. That was all.

VERWOERD. Thank you, my liefling.

She hesitates, sniffing the air discreetly .

BETSIE. I'm going to try sleeping a bit more.

VERWOERD. Yes. That's good. Lekker slaap, my lief.

*She leaves him. He retrieves the glass jar, sticks in the fork
and eats a pickled herring, pensively.* LINTWURM
appears, watching BETSIE.

LINTWURM. It's sweet – they love one another so much. And
she's so darem cute! Even with that dark complexion. It
can't be true, the rumours . . .

He winks. BETSIE *hesitates – examining the skin on her
hands anxiously – then exits.* LINTWURM *helps set up the
next scene, singing:*

LINTWURM. All things bright and beautiful
All creatures great and small . . .

Scene 4

. . . The cast join LINTWURM, *becoming a* CONGREGATION
of The Christian Church in the Daniels home – led by FATHER
DANIELS *and* HELEN *– a circle of Cape Coloured people,
holding hands and singing,* TSAFENDAS *loudest of all:*

CONGREGATION. All things wise and wonderful
The Good Lord made them all!

FATHER DANIELS. Thank you brethren, thank you. Now as
we wind up proceedings let's please just say welcome to
our new brother again . . .

CONGREGATION. Welcome Brother Demetrios . . . welcome,
welcome . . .

TSAFENDAS (*beaming*). Oh thank you, obrigada, dankie, dankie . . .

HELEN *hands round cookies, looking proud as* TSAFENDAS *launches into one of his highspeed monologues:*

TSAFENDAS. . . . As I've said all over the globe, brethren, on the beach in Greece where I was baptised a year or so ago, at the college in Turkey where I was, by the way, Professor of English, at Hyde Park Corner in London, and at their Anti-Apartheid rallies in Trafalgar Square . . .

FATHER DANIELS *frowns. He studies* TSAFENDAS *more closely.*

TSAFENDAS. . . . One day we'll all be bastards! Blacks and whites will meet in the bedroom, and God will look down and it will be good. A nation . . . no, a continent of bastards. Because we mustn't be fooled into calling ourselves Mozambicans there, or South Africans here, or whatever. We're all just Africans, African bastards, Cape Town to Cairo! We'll have a lovely blank flag one day. With a rainbow on it. A rainbow of colours. God bless us. God bless the United States of Africa! God bless the bastards! Thank you.

The CONGREGATION *exchange glances, then one or two clap politely.*

FATHER DANIELS (*worried*). Thank you Brother Demetrios. . . thank you brethren . . . same time next week, God bless you till then, goodbye en totsiens.

As the group disperses, LINTWURM *quickly signals to* TSAFENDAS – 'Look out, here's trouble!' – *and is gone.* TSAFENDAS *doesn't know what to do.* FATHER DANIELS *approaches him.*

FATHER DANIELS. Brother Dem . . . uh . . . Mister Tsafendas . . .

He hesitates, wondering how to put it. Offers a cigarette.

TSAFENDAS. Thank you kind brother, but I don't – don't smoke, don't drink, don't fornicate out of wedlock – but thank you, bless you, allow me . . .

He takes the matches from FATHER DANIELS *and lights his cigarette.*

FATHER DANIELS. Uh . . . thanks . . . agh pardon me hey, this is rather damn difficult . . . I wonder if I can see your ID please?

TSAFENDAS. My ID?

FATHER DANIELS. Ja – you got it on you?

TSAFENDAS *produces a tangle of weathered documents from his pockets, and reluctantly hands over his ID card.*

FATHER DANIELS. As I thought. 'White.' This is very difficult for us man, you must understand that.

TSAFENDAS *bows his head.*

FATHER DANIELS. On Wednesdays there's a meeting over in Newlands for, y'know, your people . . . maybe you should try there? I'm sorry.

FATHER DANIELS *exits.* TSAFENDAS *looks round for* LINTWURM, *who is nowhere to be seen. But* HELEN *is still there, staring at him, baffled. He ducks his head, and scoffs the remaining cookies from her tray.*

TSAFENDAS. D'you know something – this country isn't Christian. We're in a heathen land – did you know that? I can't pray where I want. I've prayed all over the globe. Everywhere. You name it – I've prayed there. And now I'm at the very tip of Africa, the tip of the civilised world, the pinnacle of all that modern man has achieved, and d'you know what – I can't pray where I want!

HELEN. I'm sorry Mister Tsafendas.

TSAFENDAS. Everyone's sorry. I'm sorry too, baie jammer, asminhas desculpas!

HELEN. But mixed worship's most a terrible crime. And not only praying under the same roof, but staying here too. Praying and staying. Ooh gracious me, haai shame, such trouble for us all . . .

TSAFENDAS. No, no . . . (*Packing his cases.*) I'll go to a boarding house for now.

HELEN. I wish it wasn't like this, hey?

TSAFENDAS. Me too, Miss Daniels. But I'll be back,
   I promise.

HELEN. But how? If you're -

TSAFENDAS. Look – (*Holds up ID card.*)– this is actually all
   wrong . . . I can't explain just yet . . . but trust me,
   everything will be okeydokee. It has to be. I've spent my
   whole life waiting for this. To get here, to find you.
   Penelope.

HELEN. I'm Helen.

TSAFENDAS. Hmn? No, no, she's from another story. She
   caused the whole to-do, she's the face that launched a
   thousand ships. Mind you . . . your face could also launch
   a ship or two . . .

   *She blushes, puzzled but pleased. Music is heard from the
   neighbour's radio.*

TSAFENDAS. Listen – God's whistling at us again.

HELEN. Haai . . . ! (*As he picks up his suitcases*) So I'll wait
   to hear from you hey.

   *He blows a kiss. She returns it. He exits. She exits. The
   shrill bell starts ringing in the distance again. A match
   ignites in the shadows.* LINTWURM *comes forward
   smoking.*

LINTWURM (*to audience*). When it happens, the deed, the
   cops are gonna have a corpse and a culprit – both clearly
   identifiable – and loads of witnesses too, and yet it's gonna
   stay a kinda mystery. A murder mystery, you could say.
   Why did he do it? Was he mad? Was he political? Working
   for the KGB, the CIA? (*Indicates where* HELEN *exited.*)
   Or was it because of the girl? Or-or-or . . . and this is the
   one that's really gonna grab the news . . . was it because
   someone, or something, was talking to him, driving him to
   unspeakable evil? (*Grins.*) Y'see . . . when Demetrios was
   just a teenager, and living in Lourenco Marques, one fine
   day he was taken to the doctor's . . .

Scene 5

. . . DR GOMES' consulting room: a rusty fan whirs overhead, the sound of surf drifts through Venetian blinds. GOMES is Portuguese, amiable, sozzled. A blowsy woman, MARIKA, brings in YOUNG TSAFENDAS and leaves.

DR. GOMES. . . . So OK Demetri, from what your mother tells me . . . (YOUNG TSAFENDAS *starts to protest.*) . . . sorry, *stepmother* . . . from what your stepmother says, all this eating, eating, eating, but getting thinner, thinner, thinner . . . I think this is a tapeworm you've got. You get him from bad meat. And then he grows in your gut. He is a worm, a real worm, but can he grow! Ola! 15, 20 feet! Just think of this creature in your gut, Demetri!

YOUNG TSAFENDAS *shifts in his chair, turning pale.*

DR. GOMES. Now there are two species, OK? If it's taenia saginata, I just give you some medicine, he breaks into segments, you pass these out with your stool, and that's it – esti tudo bem! – wipe your bottom Demetri, wash your hands, your troubles are over.

YOUNG TSAFENDAS *starts to relax.*

DR. GOMES. That's if it's taenia saginata. Our other friend's a little bit nastier . . .

YOUNG TSAFENDAS *tenses as* DR GOMES *pulls down a big roll-up diagram.*

DR. GOMES. Meet taenia solium. Here is one muito, muito bad fellow. You'll get him from pork – pork specifically – bad or raw pork. Now his lifespan is incredible, it's unbelievable, it can be up to twenty-five years . . . !

YOUNG TSAFENDAS *turns to the audience and mouths: 'Twenty-five years!!!'*

DR. GOMES. And that's only the start of it, alas. Por que? Because the big problem with taenia solium is that he can get into the blood, he can poison the host creature – that's you Demetri – he can affect your muscles, even paralyse them, but worse – muito, muito worse – he can affect your brain . . .

YOUNG TSAFENDAS *sways forward, head between his knees.*

DR. GOMES. . . . And then we're talking disequilibrium, failure of vision, enlargement of cerebral tisses, ah let's just call it a brain tumour.

YOUNG TSAFENDAS *slumps in a dead faint.*

DR. GOMES. Esta bem, Demetri? Take some deep breaths my boy . . .

YOUNG TSAFENDAS *stirs.*

DR. GOMES. That was just the bad news. The good news is he can also pass straight out of you. As long as you make sure of one thing. Did the *head* come out? If the head isn't out he starts growing again. And trouble is, look at this head – like a fellow wearing goggles, ah? – but pin size. A pin head. Now imagine looking for this in your stool. You're searching in there, you're digging among your stools, you're splashing about, it's the filthiest, smelliest, stinkingest pile of . . .

YOUNG TSAFENDAS *starts to sway again.*

DR. GOMES. It's OK, only joking Demetri – *I'll* do the searching! All you must do is this. You've finished your business OK, you get a bucket, you bring it to me. You do this, I find the head, your troubles are over. You don't do this . . . for the rest of your life, Demetri, you'll never know. A pain, a headache, or worse – is it you, or is it him?

DR GOMES *jerks the diagram and it rewinds with a startling snap! LINTWURM is standing behind it, wearing his goggles: a dead ringer for taenia solium. Grinning, he sinks out of view. The lights change, music starts, and the scene continues in dumbshow. YOUNG TSAFENDAS' seat is now a loo. He squeezes with all his might. Wipes, fastens his trousers, and peers back into the bowl. Amazement and relief. He calls for MARIKA. She runs in, looks, staggers back, gagging. He searches for a bucket. She reaches for the*

toilet chain. He cries 'No!' A big struggle ensues. She wins.
Pulls the chain. A flushing noise. It grows into thunder:
great cracks of it, forks of lightning too. MARIKA *strikes*
up a pose – the Wicked Stepmother. As the scene fades, we
hear GOMES' *voice echoing:*

GOMES. For the rest of your life you'll never know – is it you
or is it him?

TSAFENDAS *and* LINTWURM *enter quietly singing and*
dancing:

TSAFENDAS /LINTWURM.
Me and my shadow
Strolling down the avenue
Me and my shadow
All alone and feeling blue . . .

The CAST *hum along. The music gradually changes. Now*
everyone sings the old South African anthem, 'Die Stem' . . .

Scene 6

. . . *A government office.* VERWOERD *takes his place on an*
upper level, inside a giant gilt frame, becoming the official
portrait of the Prime Minister – a Big Brother presence
overlooking the scene. Below is a desk with chairs.
TSAFENDAS *enters with his suitcases. He sits, staring at the*
skin on his hands. KRIEL *approaches – an Afrikaner, a small*
clerical type, very anally retentive.

KRIEL. Erhm . . .

He measures TSAFENDAS' *nose with a special instrument,*
then meticulously writes notes on an official form with
carbon copy.

KRIEL. Can you please just . . .

TSAFENDAS *parts his lips.* KRIEL *measures them. Writes*
notes.

KRIEL. And, dankie, just finally . . .

He inserts his pen into TSAFENDAS' *curly hair.*

KRIEL. Shake your head 'sseblief. Harder please. Dankie.

He retrieves the pen, wipes it and writes notes. Sits at the desk.

KRIEL. And your ID please.

TSAFENDAS *hands over his ID card.* KRIEL *checks it.*

KRIEL. Well. It's very unusual, as you no doubt know, for anyone to apply *this* way round. You do understand hey? What you might end up forgoing?

TSAFENDAS (*unguardedly; like he talks to anyone*). Forgoing? Oh no sir, nothing to forgo. I've met this girl, you see. Actually she's been waiting for me for many, many years. And now we want to finally . . . y'know.

KRIEL *gives a disapproving sniff and glances up at the* VERWOERD *'portrait'.* TSAFENDAS *also looks up.* VERWOERD *remains impassive.*

KRIEL (*to* TSAFENDAS). . . . So – with regard to your racial mixture, what authorized proof, if any, do you possess?

TSAFENDAS. Papers . . . in the, y'know, record offices in . . . uhm . . . was eighteen when I looked them up. Quite a shock. To find you weren't what you thought you were. Up until then thought my looks were just a bit . . . Mediterranean . . . (*Gets lost, staring at his hands again.*) . . . But certain things fell into place now. Certain words said at school . . . (*Checks himself as* KRIEL *looks up impatiently.*) Sorry, yes, my biological mother was mulatto, as we used to call them . . .

KRIEL. Coloured.

TSAFENDAS. Coloured yes. A servant in my father's house. Apparently. I never actually knew her myself . . .

KRIEL (*writing again*). And going by the name of?

TSAFENDAS (*tenderly*). Amelia Williams.

KRIEL. Williams, A . Your father's full name?

TSAFENDAS. Michaelis Tsafandakis. Cretan. You can put Greek.

KRIEL. But – white?

TSAFENDAS. Yes. Oh yes.

KRIEL (*writing carefully*). So you're 'Greek'.

TSAFENDAS. Yes but well no – sorry – I was born in Mozambique.

KRIEL (*scratching out and writing*). . . . 'Mozambican'.

TSAFENDAS. But actually I was sent away soon after birth . . . (*Making light of it.*) Papa was a bit ashamed, I think – of his little bastard, his little half-caste bastard – so yes, sent away to live with my granny in Alexandria in, in, in Egypt, and . . .

KRIEL (*stops writing*). Listen – just state your country of residence!

TSAFENDAS. Country of residence? . . . well after Alexandria I came back – was still quite small – came back to Mozambique . . .

KRIEL *starts writing again.*

TSAFENDAS. No no, sorry – y'see, Papa had a proper wife by then, and proper children – so not very welcome again, I'm afraid, so then I was sent here, to South Africa.

KRIEL. Tsk!

All the scratching out has spoilt the carbon copy. KRIEL *prepares a new form, adding the carbon paper and duplicate copy with a ferocious 'thump' on the stapler!* TSAFENDAS *jumps.*

KRIEL (*writing*). Right – 'South Africa'.

TSAFENDAS. Yes, but well – sorry – it was only boarding school – Middelburg in the Transvaal – no, I went back to Mozambique after.

KRIEL. Right, so – 'Mozambique'.

TSAFENDAS. Well yes but then my family moved to South Africa for good and I followed them.

KRIEL (*writing fast*). Right – so – country of residence –
'South Africa'!

TSAFENDAS. Yes sir, correct. Until I went to America.

KRIEL. Arghh . . . !

Another spoilt form. Muttering angrily in Afrikaans, KRIEL
bends over to search a drawer for more stationery.
LINTWURM *immediately pops out from* TSAFENDAS'
belly (i.e. under the desk).

LINTWURM (*to* KRIEL). You poes, you prick, he's trying to
explain, he's doing his best, you pen-pushing, poes-pricking
fuck!

TSAFENDAS. Shush!

He pushes LINTWURM *out of sight as* KRIEL *looks up
from his side.*

KRIEL. What? What did you say?

TSAFENDAS. Nothing. The pollen. Tshushh! Sorry.

KRIEL *scowls at* TSAFENDAS *as he prepares another
form – 'thump' on the stapler!*

KRIEL. Right – America.

TSAFENDAS. Yes, this was during the war sir, 1942, the New
World for a new life . . .

KRIEL. Stop! Now listen carefully – just tell me – what is
your home address?

TSAFENDAS. Ah now there's a good question, sir. And one
that I've been trying to answer myself this past quarter
century, travelling the globe, on my own odyssey, my
pilgrimage whither knows where, my Great Trek, searching,
searching for that very thing. That home address.

KRIEL (*writing viciously*). 'Of no fixed abode.'

LINTWURM *pops up.*

LINTWURM. You poes, you think we like living outta fucking
suitca . . . !

TSAFENDAS. Shush!

He pushes LINTWURM *down.* KRIEL *looks up.*

KRIEL. What?

TSAFENDAS. Tshushh! (*Blowing his nose.*) 'Skuustog meneer.

LINTWURM (*up again; to* KRIEL). You poes! D'you know how many poeses like you we've known!

TSAFENDAS. Shush!

KRIEL. What?!

TSAFENDAS. No, not *you*.

LINTWURM. Yes *you*! You pussy poes-poes!

KRIEL. What?!!

LINTWURM. Pooooeess!

TSAFENDAS. Shush – please – shush . . . !

> TSAFENDAS *covers his ears as the* CAST *flood onstage babbling in different languages, all carrying suitcases.* TSAFENDAS *grabs his own cases, eyes wide, hallucinating. Lights fade on* KRIEL *and the 'picture' of* VERWOERD . . .

Scene 7

. . . *And so begins* The Ballet of the Suitcases, *a speeded-up sequence in which* TSAFENDAS *and the* CAST *play out his travels, using suitcases to create boats, desks, stairs, cells, etc. It's like a routine from an old silent comedy. There might be music, but the main soundscape is muttering and chanting:* TSAFENDAS *forever trying to explain himself at different borders, while various* OFFICIALS *and* POLICEMEN *refuse him entry or lock him up. National flags appear. Calendar dates flash by: 1942. 1943, 1944. . . etc. An array of khaki caps, fur hats, Arab head-dresses and fezzes are popped on and off by the* OFFICIALS. *They chatter away in every language under the sun. It's the Tower of Babel. And over it all, a non-stop commentary from* LINTWURM:

LINTWURM. . . . Sails to Canada, jumps ship, enters America illegally, arrested, deported. Years and years at sea, arrives in Greece, then Paris, then Lisbon, arrested, set free, back to Lourenco Marques, refused entry into South Africa, deported back to Lisbon, arrested on Spainish border, jailed, released, goes to Germany, locked up in madhouse, released, returns to Lisbon, tries to walk back to Africa, via the Balkans, Turkey, Lebanon, Syria . . .

. . . 1957, 1958, 1959 goes the calendar. On '1960' everyone freezes – except VERWOERD,*who stirs in his giant gilt frame.*

LINTWURM. Phew. Falling through the years. And now, yeah man, it's the birth of the sixties . . .

VERWOERD (*slowly*). Nineteen sixty.

LINTWURM. . . . For the world it's gonna be the decade of decadence. But not back in ol' SA of course, where our other friend's running the show . . .

VERWOERD (*standing*). Nineteen sixty.

LINTWURM. . . . There things start as they mean to go on, with – guess what? – yup, it's that word again, mm-mmm, sweet and sticky, like blood in the mouth. Ass-as-sin-nation . . .

Scene 8

LINTWURM. . . . We're at the Rand Easter Show folks, in Milner Park Joburg, on a sunny Saturday afternoon . . .

The sound of a holiday crowd and an Afrikaner band with squeezebox playing 'Sarie Marais' and other favourites.

LINTWURM. . . . Over in the Agricultural Grounds, agh kyk nou, here the visitor may marvel at giant pumpkins, golden wheat, nice fluffy sheep, great glistening bulls, and of course the fattest fucking pigs in the land . . .

Lights reveal VERWOERD *at a microphone – the giant gilt frame has become the showground stand.* BETSIE *sits*

behind him listening, bright-eyed and alert, while the other
RAND SHOW DIGNITARIES *are struggling to stay awake,*
heads lolling and jerking. A black FARM LABOURER
watches from the sidelines. The squeezebox music fades,
allowing us to hear:

VERWOERD. . . . Which brings me to my final point. We're
only at Easter time, but this particular year of our Lord –
nineteen sixty – has already been quite an eventful one.
In February we were graced by the visit of the British Prime
Minister, Mister Macmillan, who saw fit to make a speech
about 'the wind of change' blowing through the African
continent. And I saw fit to reply that this new African
National Consciousness mustn't only seek justice for the
black man, but also the white man, and we represent him –
we are the White State Of Africa – this is both our identity
and our duty. In March there was that unfortunate incident
at Sharpeville Police Station when a small but brave group
of our law enforcers were besieged by a riotous mob of
Communists and other criminals, and in the ensuing fray
some of the troublemakers were regrettaby killed – an
incident that has been, of course, grossly misreprsented by
the overseas press. I can only tell you that the history of
South Africa reveals one crisis after another, and out of each
crisis a greater triumph is born. Therefore it is fitting at this
time, this Easter time of resurrection and renewal, that I say
to you. We will never be defeated, we will always fight on,
we will survive, we-will-survive. (*A little laugh.*) And now –
in case you thought I'd forgotten – I declare the Rand Show
open! Thank you.

Big applause. The squeezebox band strikes up loudly. As
VERWOERD *sits a* MAN *rushes out of the audience,*
draws a small pistol and fires point-blank into his right
cheek – bang! – flesh spraying away. He fires a second shot
into the right ear – bang! – and is flecked with blood.
The squeezebox music continues, oblivious to the drama,
so we watch the scene in dumbshow. The black FARM
LABOURER *steps closer, amazed, stifling a yell of joy.*
Meanwhile BETSIE *and* DIGNITARIES *slowly rise in*
shock. Verwoerd's BODYGUARD *stands, fumbling for his*

*gun, then suddenly faints. People jump, thinking he's been
shot too. Then the* MAN *is overpowered. As he's turned
round, we see him for the first time – a well-to-do white
man . . .*

LINTWURM. A white bloke, a bloke called David Beresford
Pratt, born in the UK, but came here aged four, now a
bigshot farmer in the Magaliesberg, a big social jawler, and
also something of a political idealist it would seem. You can
never spot 'em hey, the guys who become our ass-sa-sins.

PRATT *is hustled off. The squeezebox music fades and the
lights narrow to a tight spot on the slumped* VERWOERD,
his head cradled by a DIGNITARY. *A very long, strange
silence, with nothing happening – just the blood bubbling
from* VERWOERD's *nose as he struggles to breathe.*

Fade to black . . .

Scene 9

. . . A hospital room. VERWOERD *lies in the bed, deeply
unconscious, his face heavily bandaged.* BETSIE *is sitting
at his side, stroking his arm.*

BETSIE. . . . . What must I do? The whole country is praying
like this, begging the Lord to spare you. They want their
Leader. I just want my husband. In the end it's just things
like looks and touches, né? Private things. Secrets. Your
shame . . . *die uitlander* . . . the alien, the Hollander. How
they punish you for it, hey, how they mock you. The way
they draw you in the papers – the Pig, the Dutch Hog. But
you won't let them see the hurt they cause – you just make
yourself calmer and stronger and wiser than anyone who's
ever been. And more South African too. The alien – he has
become the veld, the Drakensburg, the rivers and the
seashores – he has become South Africa. And nobody but
me knows how sometimes he still longs for home, the home
of his blood. (*Allows herself a smile.*) You think I can't
smell those jars you hide away? You think I don't know how

much you smaak the taste of that funny fish? A taste, a smell . . . this can bring it back, né? . . . the Amsterdam you left long ago. It's alright, my love, these things, they're in the blood. (*Her tone hardens.*) But in my blood . . . what's in my blood? The things they say. Shame on them, siss! Yet you stand by me, you never swerve, you never will. Even if tomorrow, if the unmentionable happened . . . if, say, some papers came to light and if, say, I was . . . (*Examines the skin on her hands.*) . . . even then you'd still somehow stay at my side. I think you would. Hey?

She really wishes he could answer. But he doesn't stir. She checks if he's still breathing. Only just. Covering her eyes, she prays.

BETSIE. Ooh liewe Here, liewe Vader, I'll give you ten years of my own life, twenty, thirty, I'll give our children's lives, or take one of our grandchildren – forgive me for even thinking this – but go on – een van die kleinkinders – let that be our sacrifice. But don't take *him*. Ooh liewe Jesus, help me, I didn't know a person could feel like this. Aai jirra, aai foitog . . . (*She takes deep breaths.*) Huh-uhn, whatever happens, it is God's will. And God does not make mistakes.

She prays again, softly singing the Afrikaner hymn, 'Prys die Heer met blye galme'. Her voice is gradually drowned by a distant jabber coming from the distance . . .

. . . And The Ballet of the Suitcases *arrives – a flurry of suitcases, flags and papers,* TSAFENDAS *and* OFFICIALS *talking and tumbling in the midst – the procession acting as a wipe as the scene changes . . .*

Scene 10

. . . The Ballet of the Suitcases steadies . . . though not altogether . . . this is still TSAFENDAS' *POV . . . he's swaying on his feet, exhausted and battered by his travels, carrying a mess of crumpled travel documents.*

LINTWURM . . . And in this time of moerse groot drama and
crisis folks, guess where we find our ol' pal Demetrios?
(*Croons.*) 'A foggy day in London town, it had me low
and it had me down' . . . Yup, he's turned up in London
town and headed straight for the place that's a lil' bit like
home from home . . . agh jaaa, South Africa House . . . in
Trafalgar Square . . . !

*He cues a sound effect: a big Trafalgar Square
demonstration. Chants of 'Sanctions – sanctions now –
sanctions – sanctions now' and 'Sharpeville – justice –
Sharpeville – justice' etc . . .*

LINTWURM: I tell you my outjie, out there even the pigeons
are anti-apartheid.

*The chanting continues in the background. The scene is in
the Visa Office. TSAFENDAS has spread out his documents
on the counter. This is manned by CLOETE, another grim
little South African clerk, today holding back great emotion
because of the news of the Verwoerd shooting. A queue of
British APPLICANTS wait patiently behind TSAFENDAS,
among them a young CITY GENT. LINTWURM watches
from the back.*

CLOETE. . . . But nee-wat, look here man, you're on the Stop
List!

TSAFENDAS. Am I . . . ?

CLOETE. I think you know you are Mr Tsafendas since prior
to your arrival here in the UK you've made visa applications
at our consulates halfway round the damn world!

TSAFENDAS. Have I . . . ? Yes but no, y'see, their
information about me, it's always so mixed-up . . .

CLOETE. No, no, I think their information is always very
straightforward and clear, hey. (*Referring to his own file as
well as TSAFENDAS' documents.*) You were deported from
America – an illegal immigrant, a Communist – your
temporary Portuguese passport is long since expired, ditto
your Greek travel papers, you're also banned from
Mozambique – a Communist, a draft dodger – and you . . .

TSAFENDAS. OK, now like this Communist business, let me just . . .

CLOETE. . . . And you've been held in prisons, held in asylums, deported again and again. And you were certainly registered as an Undesirable Alien on our own Stop List from as far back as 1951, when . . .

TSAFENDAS. OK wait, wait – sorry – a Stop List is like, like, like traffic lights . . . stop! go! . . . a person can't talk to traffic lights . . . but you're not, not traffic lights, so please . . . can I just . . . ? Y'see, I've been travelling for a while, quite a while, and I must go home now. And yes, you could well ask, looking at all . . . (*His papers.*) . . . why SA? Well . . . I was schooled there, y'see, and my family live there, yes, and they write all the time . . . (*He scrabbles through papers.*) . . . uhm, tsk, where's . . . ? (*Finds a small book.*) 'Turkish Phrases and ' . . . I was Professor of English, y'know, in, in, in . . . (CLOETE *isn't impressed.*) Anyway, home is where the heart is . . . good old SA . . . so that's where I must go now.

CLOETE (*impassive*). Mr Tsafendas. Even in normal times you'd be refused a visa. In the present circumstances there is absolutely no . . .

TSAFENDAS. What present circum . . . ?

CLOETE. The Prime Minister . . . the assassination . . .

TSAFENDAS. The what . . . ?

He gets a pang of stomach pain. LINTWURM *leans forward. From the demonstration outside, a single ringing cry.*

TSAFENDAS. . . . Ass . . . sa . . . si . . . nation . . .

CLOETE (*emotional*). Well – assassination attempt. But they say he can't . . . nee, maagtig! A gun. Close range. Now if you'll . . .

TSAFENDAS. Shame, poor old Smuts, and he was such a good sort, hey.

CLOETE. What . . . ?

TSAFENDAS. Oh yes he was! A war hero, a statesman par excellence . . .

CLOETE. General Smuts passed away ten years ago.

TSAFENDAS. Get away! Did he? He was PM when I left . . .

CLOETE. Well, it is Dr Verwoerd now, or it *was* . . . (*Fights back tears.*)

Suddenly a missile is thrown against the window. Everyone in the queue ducks and laughs nervously. Outside a new chant starts up: 'Let apartheid die – with Verwoerd – apartheid die – with Verwoerd' etc. CLOETE shouts towards the demonstration:

CLOETE. Jou duiwels! Jou vuilgoed! On a day like this! A day of mourning, of . . .

Everyone is staring. He controls himself, then calls past TSAFENDAS:

CLOETE. Next.

TSAFENDAS. But wait, wait, who did this . . . assassination . . . ?

CLOETE. It's in the papers, read for yourself. Next!

The young CITY GENT – fresh from public school – leans forward, showing TSAFENDAS his copy of The Times.

CITY GENT. Chap called Pratt.

The CITY GENT suppresses giggles. As do others in the queue.

TSAFENDAS. Pratt . . . ?

More giggling. CLOETE becomes upset again.

CLOETE (*to* CITY GENT). Yes sir . . . and what can I . . . ?

TSAFENDAS (*to* CLOETE). No wait, wait, wag-'n-bietjie, let's just hold our horses here, it doesn't seem fair, just because the Prime Minister has been assassinated by this Pratt . . .

Increased giggling from CITY GENT *and the queue.*

TSAFENDAS. . . . because of this, I'm refused entry into the country!

CLOETE. No, that's not the reason, en jy weet, né? (*To* CITY GENT.) Yes sir?

TSAFENDAS stays at the desk, gripped by stomach pains, while the CITY GENT *comes to the desk.*

CITY GENT (*to* CLOETE). Thank you. I've come to collect my . . . (*Starts giggling again.*) So sorry, but . . . 'prat' . . . d'you not have that word in South Africa.

CLOETE (*coldly, upset*). No sir, we do not.

CITY GENT. Here we . . . sorry . . . we say 'Don't be a prat' . . . but I suppose this chap had no choice . . . !

He dissolves in laughter. The whole queue joins in. CLOETE *starts to cry. The room is full of shaking, spluttering people. Outside the noise of the demonstration grows distorted.* TSAFENDAS *frowns – is this the normal world?*

TSAFENDAS. Pardon me . . . but I really must ask for some help now, some co-operation . . . from the authorities . . . or from . . . someone . . . !

His body also begins to shake – maybe laughter, maybe tears. LINTWURM *entwines with him. They wail together. The office dissolves.into darkness, and a giant cartoon or effigy of Verwoerd is carried into view high off the ground. He has grotesque pig features. From all around, hands pelt him with missiles. Then* LINTWURM *orchestrates everyone back into* The Ballet of the Suitcases, *and it tumbles away as the scene changes to . . .*

Scene 11

. . . The Prime Minister's Office in South Africa, five weeks later. VERWOERD *is at his desk, wearing a dressing on the right side of his face.* DR. GAVRONSKY, *chief government psychiatrist – middle-aged, Jewish, cautious – sits opposite with a file.*

GAVRONSKY. . . . So yes, a history of epilepsy certainly, and yes some evidence of depression, but nothing chronic.

Instead he just struck me as rather . . . political. During my examination he'd say things like . . . 'This policy of world isolation is leading us into the wilderness, not the promised land' . . . 'I felt what I can only call a violent urge to shoot apartheid, this snake that has us by the throat, this stinking monster that . . . ' (*He falters, feeling* VERWOERD's *gaze drilling into him.*) . . . To sum up, Prime Minister I would have to report that Pratt is an extremely well-educated, articulate . . .

VERWOERD. Pratt is mad.

GAVRONSKY. That's not altogether what I found, Prime Minister.

VERWOERD. Then you haven't looked hard enough. I trained in Psychology, doctor. I know my madmen.

GAVRONSKY. Yes Prime Minister.

VERWOERD. This one shows clear signs of megalomania. He sees himself as a political prophet, a saviour. He thinks he knows what's best for South Africa. What could be madder than that?

GAVRONSKY stares at VERWOERD, *unable to answer. Luckily* VORSTER *hurries in now. In comparison to* VERWOERD, *he's a hack-politician, beefy and boozey, a bit of a thug.*

VERWOERD. Ah good yes, come join us. Mister Vorster – Doctor Gavronsky, our chief psychiatrist.

They shake hands. VORSTER *sits – a little unsure why he's here – and gives* VERWOERD *a hastily wrapped gift.*

VORSTER. Was meant as a little get-well pres . . . but I think I'm too late . . . hell man, you're looking terrific! Isn't he looking terrific, doctor?

GAVRONSKY. Terrific.

VERWOERD. Thank you. In fact, I'm better than ever. Literally. My surgeon is going round telling this little joke. He says – 'That gun, that tiny gun, it was just what the doctor ordered. It cleared out Verwoerd's sinuses.'

VORSTER (*laughs, then hesitates*). No but what I wanna know is – why the hell did he use such a tiny little gun? .

VERWOERD. You'd've preferred something bigger?

VORSTER. Agh man, you know what I'm saying. 22 calibre. Any kid would know better. And this is a farmer. Who knows guns. Why go use a .22?

GAVRONSKY. Well, he claims it's because . . .

VERWOERD (*cutting in*). It's because he's mad.

VORSTER. Oh. (*To* GAVRONSKY.) Is that the official . . . ?

VERWOERD (*before* GAVRONSKY *can answer*). Yes it is.

VORSTER. Oh. Well. Makes life easier. No trial.

VERWOERD. No, no, of course we must have a trial – we're not barbarians. We must have a trial, and at this trial he must be found mad. Any other verdict might inflame further unrest. (*Turns to* GAVRONSKY.) So please think where you'll want him – which asylum – with a secure unit obviously – and it must be permanent, yes? Thank you, Doctor Gavronsky. (GAVRONSKY *starts to go.*) Doctor – thank you.

VERWOERD *holds out his hand.* GAVRONSKY *was carrying out Pratt's file. He hands it over reluctantly. Exits.*

VORSTER. Gavronsky. Is he . . . ?.

VERWOERD. Well, it's not a Voortrekker name, is it?

VERWOERD *gives Pratt's file to* VORSTER.

VORSTER. Uhh . . . not altogether sure how this comes under Education, Arts and Science, Oom Hendrik.

VERWOERD. Of course, you're in that depar . . . ! This medication I'm . . . !

Embarrassed, VORSTER *starts to rise.* VERWOERD *beams and points one finger: caught you!* VORSTER *looks at him, intrigued.*

VERWOERD. I'm thinking of a reshuffle, Johnnie. I'm thinking especially of Justice and Police. Would've been too obvious straight after Sharpeville. Might still be too obvious. But . . . I'm thinking.

VORSTER (*conceals his pleasure, glancing at the file*). And is this bloke mad? He was grilled and grilled. Always kept to the same story. Just isn't too happy with where you're taking the country.

VERWOERD. Where *we're* taking the country.

VORSTER. Where *we're* taking it, ja.

VERWOERD. So – ?

VORSTER. So?

VERWOERD. So clearly he's mad. Or else we are.

VORSTER *thinks, nods, then indicates the file.*

VORSTER. So what d'you wanna do with this?

VERWOERD. Oh . . . now what would a Minister of Justice and Police do with it?

VORSTER. Probably mislay it somewhere in Education, Art and Science.

VERWOERD. Easy mistake to make.

They smile. VORSTER *puts the file in his briefcase.*

VORSTER (*chuckling*). You really are well again, Oom Hendrik.

VERWOERD. I really am, Balthazar Johannes, thank you. And for the gift.

VORSTER *exits.* VERWOERD *unwraps the present. Finest Imported Dutch Herrings. He leaps to his feet. Glares after* VORSTER. *Is this meant as a mockery or a kindness? He can't be sure. Glances round. Then crouches below the desk, from where we hear the noise of greedy eating. This is gradually drowned by a familiar jabber coming from the distance . . .*

. . . And The Ballet of the Suitcases *crosses the stage . . .*

Scene 12

. . . It reaches a piece of wasteland. The CAST *collapse,
becoming* DISPLACED PEOPLE *sprawled around on their
suitcases. The sounds of water and a foghorn indicate a
quayside, but the light is strange; we could be on the moon.*
TSAFENDAS *sits with* LINTWURM *in his arms, nursing
him like a mother – except that* LINTWURM *feeds from*
TSAFENDAS' *belly, making snuffling munching noises.*

TSAFENDAS. . . . Where am I? Where is this? Piraeus? Is it
Hamburg? Nein, dies ist nicht wie Deutschland. All these
harbours, docks, beaches. Always seem to be by the sea . . .
on the sea, in the sea. Touch the sea and you touch home . . .
over the horizon, somewhere, touching you back, there's
home . . . all you have to do is name it. (*Peers round.*)
Lisbon? Is this Istanbul . . . ? (*Laughs.*) That's why they
don't answer my letters! Papa and her, his wife. No-one
knows where I am – especially not me! (*Rubs his forehead.*)
All this stuff in here . . . all the stairways and stories and
doors . . . there's only one clear thing . . . this picture
I have . . . this person in Africa . . . (*Draws an outline of
Africa in the air.*). . . Africa . . . Sometimes she's here, right
at the top, in Alexandria, and she's my yia-yia, my lovely
granny. 'Andhra moi ennepe Musa' . . . sometimes she's
here, halfway down, in Lourenco, and she's my mamma,
my real mamma – Amelia Williams – and I get to meet her
at last! . . . and sometimes she's down here, at the very
bottom, and she's . . . well, she's the girl of my dreams.
Let me . . . it's so simple . . . let me get to her and I'll be
fine, I . . . (*Sings.*) ' . . . I'm half crazy all for the love of
you . . . ' Oh it's like this huge thing in me, like a balloon,
a bomb . . . ! Oh dear, oh my tummie, oh mummie. Shush
you pig . . . !

LINTWURM *has become restless. He looks up sharply.*

LINTWURM. Hey, don't be a prat.

TSAFENDAS *goes still.*

TSAFENDAS. Oh . . . yes. Why was that funny?

LINTWURM. Some words just are. In the mouth. Language, that sandwich. Taste it. Prat . . .

TSAFENDAS. Prat . . . prat . . .

The CAST *take up a low chant – 'Prat, prat, prat.' – growing in volume.* TSAFENDAS *covers his ears. The* CAST *become* INMATES *of an asylum . . .*

Scene 13

. . . Oranje Asylum, Bloemfontein. The INMATES *are grouped round chattering, rocking, scratching. A voice is heard from the corridor:*

PRATT (*off*). But I'm not mad . . . !

The INMATES *chuckle among themselves. Then one stands up and does a Neddy Seagoon impression:*

INMATE 1. I'm not mad I tell you I'm not mad, let me out of here, I demand to see a nurse, hello nurse I'm not mad, I demand to see your superior officer, hello superior officer, Sieg Heil, I'm not mad . . .

INMATE 2. I love that show, Sunday evenings, 7.15.

They lean forward and listen intently, as though to the radio.

GAVRONSKY (*off*). Mister Pratt, we met before. I'm Doctor Gav . . .

PRATT (*off*). Yes look, could you ring my attorney please, I shouldn't be here . . .

GAVRONSKY (*off*). I know, just try and relax. You have a visitor.

PRATT (*off*). A visi . . . ?

PRATT *is suddenly silenced. As he's brought in by two* ORDERLIES *we see his mouth has been taped. And he's wearing a straightjacket.* GAVRONSKY *follows him on.* PRATT *struggles.*

GAVRONSKY. Please try to relax, Mister Pratt.

He signals to the ORDERLIES. *They herd out the other*
INMATES. *Then* GAVRONSKY *also exits, eyes lowered,*
ashamed. PRATT *goes still, listening hard. Outside, we*
hear voices whispering into walkie-talkies. A man enters.
Anonymous in hat and coat. He sits on the floor beside
PRATT, *and removes his hat. It's* VERWOERD. (*Now with*
just one plaster on his right cheek.) PRATT *gives a muffled*
scream. VERWOERD *strokes his shoulder.*

VERWOERD. It's alright . . . shh, shh, calm down . . . I'm not
going to hurt you. I just want to see you. Touch you. Smell
you. It's been on my mind. Can't dislodge it. Which is
perfectly normal behaviour I'm told. In anyone who's
endured an assault. A burglary say or even something more
violent or improper. They start to think about the other
party. This other person. Who are they? Why did they do
this thing to *me*? (*Stroking him.*) But it's alright. I'm not an
Adolf Hitler. He had those executions filmed – of the men
who tried to assassinate him – they were hung with piano
wire – and then he watched the film, several times I believe.
Not my style. I'm a Christian. Which means I do believe in
heaven and hell. I do believe they're real places. (*Looks*
round the room, thinks.) Y'know, modern psychologists
claim to be able to *heal* the human brain when it's sick.
Well I'm afraid they're wrong, Mr Pr . . . may I call you
David? . . . we're not dealing with sickness, but something
a little more sinister. All of us have known the temptations
of the three creeping evils – Doubt, Fear, Indulgence. And
we can either decide to give in, or not go that way. Which
way, you ask? The way that madness lies.

PRATT *writhes.*

VERWOERD. . . . Now back in the twenties, we were taught
what was called Behaviourism. How our circumstances
make us who we are. You see, it's tremendously difficult to
alter the adult brain. But you can certainly catch one that's
still growing. Take the Bantu. And I know my Bantu – I've
visited his kraal, I've drunk from his calabash. So when
I was Minister for Native Affairs, I felt I could help him –

thanks to my training in Behaviourism – help him not
expect more from this society – *our* society – than it could
give him. So – his brain – like a dial on a wireless, or a
stove, or a fridge – I can turn it up or turn it down. And I do
this when he's young, I do this in the classroom. I cut down
his teachers, his books, his facilities. I turn down the dial of
his education. You know the old saying, hey . . . 'If you
don't educate the native you've got yourself a savage, and
if you do educate him you've got yourself a headache. But
half-educate him, and you've got yourself a servant.' Of
course the liberal press, the Communists and so on – they
say I was using the classroom to lobotomise the black man.
Lobotomise. Not a nice word . . .

VERWOERD *touches* PRATT*'s brow.* PRATT *goes rigid.*

VERWOERD. You've got a temperature, David. It's this place.
It stinks. The revolting hygiene. And morals. And you – an
intelligent cultured man, they tell me. I'm trying to imagine
if I landed up in here. How long before I start to feel mad,
or go mad, or can't tell the difference?

PRATT *stares back with terrified eyes.*

VERWOERD. David, you are living proof of the existence of
Satan. But, far more powerfully, you prove the existence of
God. Your two bullets went deep into my head. Just a
fraction this way or that . . . just touch the facial nerve, or
the joint between upper and lower jaws – oh I've become an
expert on facial anatomy, David – just puncture the carotid
artery, directly in the path of one bullet, and I'd have bled
to death before reaching hospital. Yet your bullets missed
every single spot. Why? Who was guiding their path?
The doctors called it a miracle. So did my wife and I, except
we weren't using a figure of speech. And the miracle grew.
Enemies in my party, Afrikaners who've scorned me
because I'm not bone and marrow one of them, they are
now converted. Now that I've laid down my life for them,
and risen again. And the miracle grew. Messages of
goodwill from every corner of this land, even the liberal
press, even the non-White peoples, messages which I now
can show to the world and say. 'At last do you see how

South Africa is working!' So do *you* see, David? You not only prove the existence of God, but more wonderfully you prove His relationship with me. (*Holds back emotion.*) Thank you for this talk. It was important for both of us, I think.

VERWOERD *exits suddenly.* PRATT *thrashes wildly, giving an agonised silent scream. He's held in a single spot. From the surrounding darkness, we hear:*

LINTWURM (*a radio announcer's voice*). . . . This is the SABC. David Pratt, the man who attempted to assassinate the Prime Minister Dr Verwoerd, has taken his own life in Oranje Hospital, Bloemfontein. A hospital spokesman said that Mr Pratt was found hanging in his room yesterday ˙evening. It was his fifty-second birthday . . .

A second spot finds LINTWURM *grinning.*

LINTWURM. . . . So ja, poor Pratt, he tried and failed and vrekked. Ol' Pratt goes splatt, ol' Doc. Verwoerd goes from strength to strength, and then, lo and behold, ol' Demetrios gets back into South Africa . . .

A third spot on TSAFENDAS *trudging forward with his suitcases.*

LINTWURM. . . . Don't even ask how. Some official in some consulate somewhere not checking his Stop List properly – dozy, drunk, or bored to fuckdom, who knows – but he gets back in. Was it chance? Was it meant? Is there Someone up there after all? Or Someone down below?

PRATT *and* TSAFENDAS *exchange a long strange look; one assassin passing on the job to another – even though the second is still innocent of the deed – then the spot snaps out on* PRATT. TSAFENDAS *puts down his cases.* HELEN DANIELS *enters, carrying tea and biscuits – as in Scene 2 – and we hear the little radio tune to which they danced. She walks slowly past him and exits.*

LINTWURM. . . . And then he finds the girl of his dreams – agh but you remember this bit, folks – and he runs into one helluva ID prob, and applies for reclassification, and – OK, now here's where things get weird – no results have come through yet, and that was a whole *year* ago now . . .

The sound changes to birds, trees rustling in the wind, people strolling along gravel paths . . .

Scene 14

. . . The Botanical Gardens alongside the Houses of Parliament, Cape Town. A park bench with the sign: Europeans Only, Slegs Blankes. A drunk black TRAMP *is lying sprawled on the ground, unconscious.* TSAFENDAS *stands to one side, looking around expectantly.* LINTWURM *lights a ciggie.*

LINTWURM. . . . Now is the winter. In Cape Town. That damp and drizzle, that thump of Atlantic breakers along the shore – like a line of fucking cannons, man – that foghorn keening away down at Moullie Point, and here in the Gardens, the oak trees a bit bare, colours a bit grey, and ol' Table Mountain a bit lost in the mist . . .

TSAFENDAS sees someone coming and prepares himself. LINTWURM takes the suitcases and slips away. The TRAMP snores. HELEN DANIELS arrives. She's dressed in a maid's apron and cap.

TSAFENDAS. Here you are.

HELEN. I haven't got long.

TSAFENDAS. No. But we can just have a quick bite together.

He produces sandwiches wrapped in greaseproof paper.

HELEN. I get given lunch at work.

TSAFENDAS. Oh. Okeydokee. (*Starts wolfing the sandwiches.*) Want to sit down?

HELEN. I can't.

TSAFENDAS. Sorry?

She indicates the sign on the bench.

TSAFENDAS. Oh. Sorry. Anyway, so how've you been?

HELEN. No fine thanks. You wanted to see me?

TSAFENDAS. Well . . . yes of course . . . been wanting to see you ever since . . . I saw you. (*Pause.*) I've got a new job. (*Pause.*) Give you a clue. I'll be wearing a uniform. Dark blue.

HELEN. Bus conductor.

TSAFENDAS. Bus cond . . . ? No! Parliamentary messenger. Right over there, right in parliament. Me. Among the great and good of the land. Me!

She looks at him warily.

HELEN. And how did you go get a job like that?

TSAFENDAS (*whispers confidentially*). I don't know. (*Laughs.*) Went for the interview, thought there's no chance, they'll check on all my . . . y'know . . . but I don't think they checked anything! Apparently it's a job that's normally done by a rather lowly type of person. So maybe, y'know, with all my languages and so on . . . Anyhow – hey presto – I start on Monday!

HELEN. So. May you have health and happiness in your new job, Master Demetrios.

Slight pause.

TSAFENDAS. What did you just call me?

She lowers her head.

TSAFENDAS. I can't believe you just said that. It's *me*.

HELEN. No it isn't Master . . .

TSAFENDAS. Don't keep saying . . .

HELEN. . . . When we saw one another last you said everything will be OK, you said I must trust you, you said you'd be back. But that was a year ago and you haven't been back. Or at any rate, ja you're probably back with your own people.

TSAFENDAS. No, no . . . just been in different rooms, different jobs. Alright look, let me tell you, months ago

I went to the Population Registry people, and applied for reclassification. I should never have been 'White' on my card. My mother was Coloured, you see, so . . . 's all just a mix-up.

She looks up, full of hope.

HELEN. And – ?

TSAFENDAS. Well, it takes time, you see, all the paperwork and procedures, but I'm still jolly sure that any day now a letter will arrive and . . .

HELEN. So – pardon me – in the meantime you're still 'White'?

TSAFENDAS. Well yes. But it's just a mix-up.

HELEN. A mix-up in writing. A mix-up in black and white. A mix-up that looks like a fact.

TSAFENDAS. Alright. We just ignore it. We rip it up. (*Takes out his mess of papers and documents, and finds his ID card.*) You want me to rip it up?

HELEN. No! It's against the law!

TSAFENDAS (*laughing gently*). Oh Miss Daniels. Dear Miss Daniels. 'Against the law.' I've spent most of my life against the law, and look at me – do I seem like a criminal, a bad character? The law just doesn't always fit everyone. It doesn't fit me.

HELEN. How d'you mean?

TSAFENDAS. Well, it's like me and the Communist Party . . .

HELEN. You and the Communist . . . ?!

TSAFENDAS. Yes but not like . . . it was just . . . handing out a few leaflets, watching some filmshows . . . it was warm in those rooms, it was chatty, it was just, y'know, friendship. But it's 'against the law', the Communist Party, so now suddenly I'm 'against the law'! That's barmy. The law says I'm not even allowed in this country, I'm a banned person . . .

HELEN. You're banned?!!

TSAFENDAS. I am! (*Laughing.*) And I honestly can't even tell you how I got in. It's like this new job. Just . . . hey presto. My whole life's been full of these hey-prestos. At times it's felt like, oh, a paper in the wind, a cork on the ocean wave, a rolling stone, but anyhow here I am, and – hey presto – things are looking up!

She stares at him, frowning deeply.

TSAFENDAS. Dear Miss Daniels. The law might say we can or can't sit on that bench. I say who cares?

HELEN. I do . . . !

She erupts in anger – startling him – waking the TRAMP.

HELEN. . . . Who are you to come here, y'know, messing with my life, y'know, upsetting me like this? The Government over there, your new bosses, they say I must care about sitting on this bench – take great care Helen Daniels, they say – the Church says it too, it's even in the Bible, this bench, in the Tower of Babel story – 'And if the nations is one, if the peoples is one, then *nothing* will be restrained from them.' God Himself is warning us about this bench! So pardon me but, y'know, who on earth are you to come here and say anything different?! Oo Vader! You – a Commie, a banned person, a person who shouldn't even be anywhere near this bench in the first place!

TSAFENDAS. Miss Daniels, please . . .please just think why I'm here. It's because of you. I'm the man who's dreamed about you all his life.

HELEN. Agh man, you didn't even hear about me till the Durban brethren put us in touch . . .

TSAFENDAS. No, no, no, long before then. I've told you. My granny, in Alexandria . . . 'Andhra moi ennepe Musa' . . . the long search, I've told you all about it . . . Penelope.

HELEN (*head in her hands*). Penelope again.

TSAFENDAS. I'm just trying to say . . . she must need him too, sitting at her loom, waiting all those years . . . she must believe there's no-one else for her. You ask who I am? I'm the man who's finally found you.

She weeps. He does too. They stand there awkwardly, blowing their noses. The black TRAMP *watches them sadly.* TSAFENDAS *steps forward and tries to embrace* HELEN. *She recoils.*

HELEN. No Master!

TSAFENDAS. Don't call me . . .

HELEN. Listen to me – you mustn't be in touch again – you hear? Please – I ask you with all my heart. I'm a quiet person, I'm a respectable person. Now when we started writing, I thought . . .

TSAFENDAS. Yes I did too.

HELEN. Huh-uhn, I didn't just think – I hoped, I prayed with all my might.

TSAFENDAS. Yes, me too.

HELEN. Ja maybe. But we were wrong.

TSAFENDAS. No.

HELEN. Yes. We were just wrong. In every way. Master. Wrong.

She goes. He stands, numb with shock. LINTWURM *steps from the bushes.*

TSAFENDAS. I've heard this tune before, y'know – 'Bugger off, get lost, voetsek, desapareçe!' But no, no, I'm holding on this time. It's not over . . .

LINTWURM (*overlapping*). It is . . .

TSAFENDAS. . . . . She's not gone . . .

LINTWURM. . . . . Yes she has . . .

TSAFENDAS. . . . . Just have to be patient . . .

LINTWURM. . . . . Patient, pay-shit . . .

TSAFENDAS. . . . . Just wait for the letter . . .

LINTWURM. . . . . Forget the letter . . .

TOGETHER. . . . . Oh how can it take so long?! . . .

TSAFENDAS. . . . Never mind, just wait, just wait . . .

LINTWURM. . . . Don't wait, don't wait . . .

TSAFENDAS. . . . I wan' an ice cream . . . gimme an ice cream . . . !

LINTWURM *drives him round the stage with little shoves and light slaps of his face. The drunk* TRAMP *blinks – is he seeing or dreaming this?*

LINTWURM. C'mon buddy, we can do better than ice cream.

TSAFENDAS. No . . .

LINTWURM. Yes. Fuck ice cream.

TSAFENDAS. Ouch.

LINTWURM. . . . Let's stop waiting.

TSAFENDAS. Leave me!

LINTWURM. . . . Let's start doing.

TSAFENDAS. Don't!

LINTWURM. Don't what?

TSAFENDAS. Stop it – you pig!

He grabs LINTWURM *by the throat. The* TRAMP *flees.*

LINTWURM (*to* TSAFENDAS). Attaboy, 's more like it!

TSAFENDAS *releases him, surprised by his own violence.*

LINTWURM. Yeah, that's much, much more . . .

TSAFENDAS. Shut up! Just *shush*!

LINTWURM (*whispers*). Shush, absolutely . . . must get ready for Monday . . . shhhhh . . . we start work on Monday . . . shhh . . .

He hums or whistles 'Heigh ho, heigh ho, it's off to work we go.' The lights fade. In the distance the shrill bell rings, coming closer.

Scene 15

Tight spot on TSAFENDAS *who looks drawn and pale. He's surrounded by total darkness.*

TSAFENDAS. . . . Why did it make me feel so funny? Maybe it was just because I haven't been sleeping too well. Haven't been sleeping at all. Since she . . . uhm. Maybe it was just that. But you know how certain places burn into the brain? Maybe it's a Table Mountain or the Acroplis or whatever. For me it's often rooms. I walk in and I *know*. Me and the air and the walls and what's in them – bricks and mortar and ghosts – something mixes and mashes us all together. Rooms in boarding houses. Rooms in hospitals. Rooms in prison. Usually small rooms, small whitish rooms. This room was gigantic. And totally black at first. Yet you could smell how big it was. You know that coolness? Like inside a church. You're inside a church and you've got your eyes closed, praying say, but you can just sense all this distance, to the sides and above . . . feels like a big mystery all around. That's how it was in this room, this gigantic black room. He'd switched on the lights but nothing happened. I thought hell's bells a blown fuse *in here*. Then gradually things started to take shape . . . dark golden brown walls . . . green leather benches . . . thick carpet, with sworls and emblems . . . These lights, sort of phosphorescent lights high up on the ceiling, they were slowly, slowly showing me the room. A room I'd never seen before yet sort'f knew well. Exactly like a dream. A room I'd never leave, in a way. It was that strong. A brainstorm as much as a room. And there at the end was a kind of throne. He said this had a name . . .

SCHALK. . . . the Speaker's Chair!

The lights reveal TSAFENDAS *and a Senior Messenge,r* SCHALK, *standing in the middle of the House of Assembly in Cape Town.* LINTWURM *lurks in the shadows. It's* TSAFENDAS' *first morning in his new job – as temporary parliamentary messenger . He's still in civvies, with the dark blue uniform draped over one arm.* SCHALK – *poor*

white, a scrawny sour character – is already dressed in his
uniform. He watches TSAFENDAS' *reaction.*

SCHALK. Hey -?

TSAFENDAS. My, my.

SCHALK. The seat of government.

TSAFENDAS. Holy Moses.

SCHALK. The seat of power.

TSAFENDAS. The very nub of it.

SCHALK. The hallowest highest Chamber in the land.

TSAFENDAS. My God, 'tis Delphi itself!

SCHALK. Tis what?

TSAFENDAS. The Oracle.

SCHALK. The whatical?

TSAFENDAS. My, my, my!

LINTWURM *suddenly darts from the shadows, lowers his*
trousers and moons at the Speaker's Chair, dances
grotesquely, barks like a madman. TSAFENDAS *quickly*
masks him from SCHALK's *view.*

SCHALK. What . . . ?

TSAFENDAS. Nothing . . . 'm just . . . excited. Can't wait to
start. Thank you for showing me round . . . baie dankie . . .
(*Shakes* SCHALK's *hand.*) Ah. Wedding ring. Very nice.

SCHALK. Thatty-four bleddy years – not so nice. And you?

TSAFENDAS. Huhh? Yes, yes. Any day now in fact. Just a
teeny little hitch. Just waiting on this letter. Bit of official
business. But any moment now . . . (*Sings.*) 'It won't be a
stylish marriage, I can't afford a carriage . . . '

SCHALK. Well yous in the right place, man.

TSAFENDAS. Sorry?

SCHALK. Official business, letters, forms, and so on. This is
where they get signed and sealed. And carted round by the

likes of you and me. Messages, memos, telegrams, also tea wif sandwiches, beers for the reporters, so on 'n so forth. A job for kaffirs really, but kaffirs 's not allowed to. So Meneer T, yous gonna be it now. A kaffir. A white kaffir. How old are you hey? Never mind, they'll call you 'boy' – just like a kaffir – 'messenger boy'! (*Laughs grimly.*) You getting the picture, boy?

TSAFENDAS. Yes.

SCHALK. Sir!

TSAFENDAS. Sir.

SCHALK. OK boy, then lemme show yous the changing room . . . (*He suddenly goes still, listening.*) Jesus – fok me!

In a flash he's gone. Out the door? Behind a bench? TSAFENDAS half runs this way, then that. A MAN appears from behind the Speaker's Chair – just a silhouette for now, the light from an open door behind him.

MAN. Who's there?

TSAFENDAS. Nobody.

MAN. What?

TSAFENDAS. Just a messenger.

MAN. A messenger?

TSAFENDAS. A messenger *boy*.

The MAN comes closer. It's VERWOERD. Hair unbrushed. In shirtsleeves and braces. Carrying a fountain pen.

VERWOERD. I heard someone.

TSAFENDAS. No sir. Nobody here sir.

VERWOERD checks round, seeming to look through TSAFENDAS, then shrugs and starts to retire. TSAFENDAS suddenly rushes towards him.

TSAFENDAS. Sir!

VERWOERD stops.

TSAFENDAS. Sir, I wonder if . . .

VERWOERD *turns – an imposing figure.* TSAFENDAS *goes rigid.*

TSAFENDAS. You . . . you just working early, sir?

VERWOERD. Hmm? Working late.

TSAFENDAS. Sorry sir?

VERWOERD. What's the time?

TSAFENDAS. It's about seven-fifteen, sir.

VERWOERD. In the *morning*?

TSAFENDAS. Yes sir.

VERWOERD. Is it really? . . . Is it really?! (*He rubs his face, then looks at* TSAFENDAS *properly for the first time.*) So much still to do, so much . . .

   VERWOERD *exits.* TSAFENDAS *sways.* LINTWURM *shoots to his side.*

TSAFENDAS. I can't believe what I almost did.

LINTWURM. What?

TSAFENDAS. Can't believe it even came to mind.

LINTWURM. What?

TSAFENDAS. I almost . . .

LINTWURM. What??

TSAFENDAS. Asked for his help.

LINTWURM. His help?

TSAFENDAS. My application . . . my letter . . . my life . . . help!

   LINTWURM *opens his arms.* TSAFENDAS *buries himself in the embrace. They entwine.* LINTWURM *eyes us over* TSAFENDAS' *shoulder with a little smile. The shrill bell rings.*

   Lights fade.

   End of Act One.

ACT TWO

Scene 16

*A row of ten chairs. Facing a line of lightbulbs. It's the
messengers' corridor in the basement of the House of
Assembly. Six uniformed* PARLIAMENTARY MESSENGERS
are presently seated, TSAFENDAS *and Senior Messenger*
SCHALK *among them. Everyone's bored senseless. One or
two chat quietly. But not* TSAFENDAS. *It's several weeks
later, and he's in a bad way – possessed with peculiar stillness
– an unexploded bomb. One of the lightbulbs flashes. People
speak in whispers, like in a library:*

SCHALK. Post-room.

    MESS 1 *exits. Pause. Another light.*

SCHALK. Lobby.

    MESS 2 *exits. A light.*

SCHALK. Whip's Office.

    MESS 3 *exits.* MESS 1 *returns. A light.*

SCHALK. Floor of the House . . . oh that's me.

    SCHALK *exits.* MESS 2 *returns. Two lights.*

MESS 1. Security, Lobby.

    MESS 4 *and* 2 *exit.* MESS 3 *returns.* SCHALK *returns.
A light.*

SCHALK. Press Gallery.

    Nobody moves. SCHALK *and* MESSENGERS *whisper
together:*

ALL. Press Gallery!

TSAFENDAS. Huhh . . . ? Oh. Sorry.

    TSAFENDAS *exits right. Immediately reappears, tutting,
and exits left.* SCHALK *and* MESSENGERS *exchange*

looks. One of them mimics TSAFENDAS. *Some quiet laughter. They settle.* MESS 4 *returns.* MESS 2 *returns.* TSAFENDAS *returns. Everyone sits blank-faced. This could go on forever. The scene fades as* LINTWURM *enters, sniffing a flower.*

LINTWURM. It's Thurday the first of September, folks, 1966. Spring is coming to Cape Town. In the Gardens – just outside here, outside parliament – the long gravel-strewn avenues are growing shadier, trees are budding, flowers opening. African flowers. Huge shocking colours, sweet rotting flavours taking to the air. September will be the month of sunshine, blossom and birth. It'll also be the month of murder. And today, Thursday, is the first of that month. We've got just six days to go . . .

Scene 17

LINTWURM. . . . Six days and six nights.

Lights reveal a corner of the Docks at night: a ship's gangplank with the name 'Eleni'. Drunken voices come out of the dark. Weaving their way to the ganglank are two members of the Greek crew – the tall bosun MANOLIS *and a young sailor* NIKKI – *with a big, feisty Coloured prostitute,* DAISY. *She has her hands in their flies, they have their hands in her dress.* TSAFENDAS *is to one side, the wallflower as always, but he doesn't care. He's paralytic. A bottle and a joint are being passed around.* TSAFENDAS *is also scoffing fish and chips.*

TSAFENDAS. . . . An' here y' are . . . home sweet home.

MANOLIS. Eh, nasa kala Mimi.

NIKKI. Yeh, all thanks to the Pig – oink-oink!

EVERYONE. Oink-oink!

DAISY (*beckoning* TSAFENDAS). Come here my little piggy, let this little piggy come to market too, come here my darling . . .

TSAFENDAS (*pulling back shyly*). No, no . . .

DAISY (*to the sailors; her tone affectionate*). Agh sweet, he's keeping hisself pure for his true love – he's mos' told me – isn't that so, my darling?

TSAFENDAS. Sort of, mm . . . (*Leaving.*) See y' all.

MANOLIS. When tomorrow, Mimis? For our last night.

TSAFENDAS. 'll stroll down from parliament at 'bout five. See y' then. Oink-oink!

EVERYONE. Oink-oink!

TSAFENDAS starts to stagger away. LINTWURM is waiting for him in the shadows, very pissed too. The others are about to climb the gangplank. Suddenly a torch shines out of the shadows:

MULLER. Hey – just hold it there!

Everyone turns back. MULLER steps into view. A Harbour Policeman. Afrikaner, brutish, a real hairyback.

MULLER (*to MANOLIS and NIKKI*). And where yous think yous taking her?

NIKKI. Ai gamisou malaka! 'S none of your business, eh!

MULLER. Oh but it is, sonny. Yous white, she's not. Yous contravening the law of the land.

DAISY. Ja well we's not gonna do it on the land . . . (*Teetering onto the gangplank.*) . . . So jus' gaan fok, man! (*To MANOLIS and NIKKI.*) C'mon my darlings.

MULLER grabs her by the hair and hauls her back onto the quayside.

DAISY (*screeching*). Eina! Gaan naai, jou fokkin doos!

MULLER (*slapping her*). Hou jou fokkin bek, jou fokkin hoer!

MULLER and DAISY yell in Afrikaans, MANOLIS and NIKKI in Greek, while TSAFENDAS stumbles about between them, trying to restore peace.

TSAFENDAS. Wait a mo' . . . alright, alright . . . wha' seems to be the problem?

DAISY (*to* MULLER, *indicating* TSAFENDAS). Ja you better watch it hey – he's a big member of Parliament, hey?

MULLER. He's *what*?

TSAFENDAS. Yes I am my good sir, so less jus' watch our P's and Q's please.

MULLER (*advancing on him*). You'll watch the fokkin stars, mister.

DAISY (*screeching*). Haai leave hom jou piel, he's not doing nothing!

MULLER. Hou jou fokkin bek!

NIKKI. Eh, you don't talk to a lady like . . . !

MULLER. Now look sonny – just shut it! This isn't your country, this isn't your business, and this isn't a lady! This is a hoer! A Coloured hoer! She can't fok with any of yous!

DAISY. Agh, jou piel is Coloured, jou moer!

He slaps her several times. NIKKI *lunges forward.* MANOLIS *restrains him. But now* TSAFENDAS *suddenly staggers in front of* MULLER, *strangely aggressive –* LINTWURM *shadow-boxing nearby; a coach egging on his champion.*

TSAFENDAS. Wait – listen here – *I'll* fuck with her if I choose! What colour am I, hey, c'mon, what colour'm I?

MULLER. I'm not playing guessing games with bleddy dronkies – just gimme your fokkin ID.

TSAFENDAS. An' wha' if my fokkin ID's wrong, sunshine, wha' then?

MULLER (*grabbing him*). Then yous really in deep shit, man.

TSAFENDAS. Don't you – !

He shoves MULLER *off with real violence.* LINTWURM *shadow-boxes gleefully.* MULLER *roars and advances again.* DAISY *intervenes to protect* TSAFENDAS, *hitting* MULLER *with her shoe.*

DAISY. Los hom jou doos, he's a fokkin member of Parliament . . . !

MULLER *suddenly wheels on* DAISY *and punches her hard in the stomach. As she bends double, he knees her in the face. Teeth and blood fly. She collapses. The men watch in shocked silence.* MULLER *handcuffs the unconscious* DAISY *and, like a caveman., drags her away.*

MULLER (*shouting over his shoulder*). If any of yous fokkin dronkies is here when I gets back, yous behind bars tonight, end of story!

He's gone. The men stagger round wildy.

MANOLIS. Crazy country, eh?

TSAFENDAS. It is, is . . . 's a madhouse!

NIKKI. The Pig's right . . . 's a madhouse!

TSAFENDAS. Less go get him.

MANOLIS. Get who?

TSAFENDAS. That cop.

NIKKI. Yeh – less get him!

TSAFENDAS. Get him, kill him!

NIKKI. Kill him, yeh!

TSAFENDAS (*leading them off*). Kill, kill, kill – !

MANOLIS. Eh wait, wait – c'mon – jus' think. You don't kill someone for jus' stopping one fuck. Not even Cretans kill someone for that!

TSAFENDAS (*pushing forward; very macho*). My father was a Cretan. No-one stood in his way. So don't tell me about Cretans, eh?

MANOLIS *and* NIKKI *laugh in his face.* TSAFENDAS *goes silent.*

MANOLIS. Eh, I'm drunk . . .

NIKKI. Yeh.

MANOLIS. Less jus' go to bed.

NIKKI. Yeh.

MANOLIS. Can I jus' fuck you again?

NIKKI. OK.

MANOLIS. Easier.

NIKKI. Easier.

They start up the gangplank.

TSAFENDAS. Wait, wait, aren't we gonna go kill . . . ?

MANOLIS. No, we're gonna go fuck.

TSAFENDAS. But wait, wait . . . (*He staggers in a circle –
    drunk, confused, in strange despair.*) Everyone's fucking!
    Everyone's fucking except fucking me!

NIKKI. Yeh . . . 's a madhouse.

MANOLIS (*to* NIKKI). Jus' get to Saturday, eh.

TSAFENDAS. Sa'day? Wha' happens Sa'day?

MANOLIS *and* NIKKI (*disappearing up the ganglank*). We
    sail, Saturday . . . Cape of Good Hope . . . good riddance,
    a isto kalo! Eh Mimis, sail with us!

TSAFENDAS. No. I'm here . . .

The men are gone.

. . . I'm here now, I'm home at last. Hullo – I'm home! Oh .
    . . can't think straight . . . dunno what . . . can't, can't,
    can't . . . !

TSAFENDAS *goes onto all fours, growling with
    frustration.* LINTWURM *joins him. They entwine. Their
    noise grows. Dogs howling at the moon . . .*

Scene 18

LINTWURM. It's Friday the 2nd of September, folks.

*Seated on their row of chairs in the basement corridor,
are* SCHALK, MESSENGER 1 *and* TSAFENDAS – *who
hasn't slept at all, and is battling to hold things together.
One of the lights flashes.*

SCHALK. Post-room.

> MESS 1 *exits* . MESS 2 *returns from a previous errand. A light flashes.* SCHALK *waits till* MESS 2 *sits.*

SCHALK. Lobby.

MESS 2. Fok.

> MESS 2 *exits again. A light.*

SCHALK. Floor of the House . . . fok.

> *As* SCHALK *exits,* TSAFENDAS *leaps up and acts shooting him – with his fingers – making gun noises under his breath like a child. Stops. Puts his fingers to his temple. Fires. Acts his head exploding. Hears someone coming. Sits – trying to look normal.* SCHALK *returns. A light.*

SCHALK. Press Gallery.

TSAFENDAS. Indeed.

> TSAFENDAS *exits. A light.* SCHALK *groans and exits. Silence in the empty corridor. Then two men hurry in at one end – the* INTERIOR MINISTER *and his* JUNIOR CLERK *– needing a private word.*

INTERIOR MINISTER (*checking documents*). . . . Entered the country November '63. Yet his name was clearly on the Stop List . A Communist, a Banned Person, an Undesirable Alien. A Stop List means stop. You can't come in. Go back. This is the point of a Stop List.

JUNIOR CLERK. Ja, 's funny meneer.

INTERIOR MINISTER. Yet here's his name again – July '65 – at the Population Registry Office applying for . . . reclassification as a Coloured?! Does anyone apply that way round?

JUNIOR CLERK. 'S very funny meneer.

INTERIOR MINISTER. And here we are now – September '66 – and the Ministry of the Interior is only finding out about this *now*?!

JUNIOR CLERK. 'S bloody funny meneer.

INTERIOR MINISTER. It's bloody hilarious.

JUNIOR CLERK (*squirming*). Paperwork takes time, meneer.

INTERIOR MINISTER. Jesus. And this damn character has been waiting for an answer all this time?! Jesus Christ. Where the hell is he now?

JUNIOR CLERK. Uhm . . .

As JUNIOR CLERK *consults a file,* TSAFENDAS *re-enters and takes his seat behind them. His eyes are glazed, he's not paying attention.*

JUNIOR CLERK. . . . a room near the Docks, meneer.

INTERIOR MINISTER. And doing what kind of job?

JUNIOR CLERK (*searching the file*). Oh, he's – ! Oh no, he left that one. No, doesn't say, meneer.

INTERIOR MINISTER. OK, a deportation order – you draw it up, I sign it, police deliver it to his address.

JUNIOR CLERK. Yes meneer, straightaway meneer.

They hurry in different directions. TSAFENDAS *stares into space.* LINTWURM *comes forward, smiling.*

LINTWURM. So his deportation order was drawn up, signed and sealed, and put in an out-tray. Where it'll still be lying come Tuesday next. Agh, you know how it is – paperwork takes time.

LINTWURM *notices* TSAFENDAS' *blank stare. He touches him.* TSAFENDAS *doesn't respond.* LINTWURM *looks worried . . .*

Scene 19

TSAFENDAS' room. No furniture. Only his two suitcases. He's scoffing a chokkie bar. Finishes, unwraps another. His eating is compulsive, unstoppable. LINTWURM *is hooked on his stomach, trying to keep up, but without appetite. He turns to us bloated and burping:*

LINTWURM. It's the weekend folks . . . it's Saturday . . . it's the 3rd of September . . .

TSAFENDAS *listens. A ship's hooter is departing from the Docks. He eats noisily to drown the sound.*

TSAFENDAS (*mouth full*). Where is this?

LINTWURM. Huhn?

TSAFENDAS. Piraeus? Is this Piraeus? No. Beirut?

LINTWURM. C'mon buddy – this is Cape Town.

TSAFENDAS. Cape Town. I'm still here?

LINTWURM. 'Fraid so . . .

TSAFENDAS *wants another chokkie. Searches one of his suitcases. Nothing but empty silver wrappers, dozens of them. Waddles over to the other case, lugging LINTWURM along. TSAFENDAS finds a mouldy old hot dog. LINTWURM gags as TSAFENDAS starts consuming it. And now a half-eaten tin of beans.*

LINTWURM. For fuck's sake stop . . .

TSAFENDAS. Yes, well, it's not easy eating for two.

LINTWURM. Stop it, you pig!

TSAFENDAS. You're the pig.

LINTWURM. No – you.

TSAFENDAS. *You*. Pigmeat. Bad meat.

LINTWURM. Bad you. Called Pig. Oink-oink.

TSAFENDAS. Oink-oink-oink . . .

As TSAFENDAS digs in the cases for more goodies, some newspaper clippings fall out. LINTWURM grabs one: a cartoon of Verwoerd.

LINTWURM. And here's another Pig.

TSAFENDAS (*refusing to look*). Awful lot of pigs about. If they could fly we'd be in trouble.

LINTWURM (*thrusting the cartoon under his nose*). Except he's the real Pig! Hey? Look! There's a Pig running the country. Telling you who you can marry, can't marry.

TSAFENDAS (*getting upset*). Can love, can't love.

LINTWURM. Or even just fuck.

TSAFENDAS. Yet look at him.

LINTWURM. His own wife!

TSAFENDAS. So they say.

LINTWURM. Yet he's the big fucking bigshot. Why? Jesus
fuck man, y'know, I get blue, blue for you man. You don't,
but I do. Blue for you. I ask why the fuck is everyone else
better? Everyone in the whole fucking world. I'm sick of it
man, sick of everyone shitting on you man, shutting doors
in your face, shitting and shutting, fuck it man, I'm sick of
it! Why's this Pig better than you? He's just some prick,
some Pig prick, some Pig prick poes that you work with!
Think about it, man. You and him – you just work together,
that's all. Both just working away there in parliament,
making and shaping the nation. Fuck it man, you're so close
you can reach out and touch. Why don't you? But for real.
For real. I mean, don't be a prat.

TSAFENDAS *freezes. Looks at* LINTWURM *in fear. Then
scrabbles round for more food.* LINTWURM *grabs the
newspaper cartoons and stuffs them into* TSAFENDAS'
mouth.

LINTWURM. No – get this inside you – this pig – this fuck
pig – yeah c'mon – this pussy poes pig!

TSAFENDAS *spits out the paper.* LINTWURM *dances
round, punching him.*

LINTWURM. C'mon. Call yourself a man?

TSAFENDAS. Don't – !

LINTWURM. Call yourself a Cretan?

TSAFENDAS. Go away – get out!

LINTWURM. Call yourself your Papa's son?

TSAFENDAS *hesitates.* LINTWURM *suddenly draws a big
knife. Lunges at* TSAFENDAS *with real intent.*

C'mon – yeah – we fight with knives in Crete – big knives –
yeah – c'mon, big Cretan man – or what are you? – just the
little half-caste bastard?

*TSAFENDAS goes still at this. LINTWURM draws a
second knife – one in each hand.*

LINTWURM. C'mon – for once in your life – come on!

*TSAFENDAS explodes. Picks up one of the suitcases and
attacks LINTWURM wildly:*

TSAFENDAS. Ase me, fiye, fiye, ti xeris esi kathici yia tin
Kriti, ti xeris esi yia tou patera mou, ti xeris yia meno, fiye,
ase me!

*TSAFENDAS drives LINTWURM out of the room.
TSAFENDAS shuts the door tight. Stacks both cases
against it. Adds his own weight to the barricade. Stays
there, panting, eyes wide, frightened . . .*

Lights fade down and up again.

*. . . TSAFENDAS has fallen asleep on the barricade.
Church bells. He stirs. A knock on the door. He tenses. The
knock comes again. Gentle, unthreatening.*

TSAFENDAS. Uhm . . . who is it?

A VOICE (*off*). Special delivery. From the Population Registry
Office.

TSAFENDAS. My application . . . oh thank God . . . at last . . . !

*He drags the barricade away. Throws opens the door. A
colossal head crashes through – an insect head with
goggles – a GIANT TAPEWORM.*

GIANT TAPEWORM (*booming*). Fooled you! It's Sunday the
4th of September! It's just two days to go!

*The rest of the GIANT TAPEWORM crowds into the room –
the whole CAST doing a Chinese Dragon – and
TSAFENDAS is overwhelmed, vanishing into its twisting
coils, caught in an ultimate entwining . . . !*

Lights fade down and up again.

*. . . TSAFENDAS is lying on the floor, sucking his thumb,
eyes open, unblinking. LINTWURM sits next to him,
relaxed and smoking: an attitude of almost post-coital ease.
The GIANT TAPEWORM's head is draped over his
shoulders, the empty body trailing out the door.*

LINTWURM. It's Monday the 5th of September, folks. It's the
day before. And I think we're finally all set to go. Hey,
buddy . . . ? s

*He leans forward and whispers gently into TSAFENDAS'
ear. TSAFENDAS nods slowly. Lights fade . . .*

Scene 20

LINTWURM. Folks, this is it. Tuesday, September 6, '66.
Hey – six-six-six! The number of the Beast. Just taste them –
those sixes. Six . . . sick . . . sexxx. It is the day. The Day of
all Days. A clear spring day.

*VERWOERD comes forward in his pyjamas, looking
curiously young and innocent .*

VERWOERD. I slept like a babe – which isn't like me – slept
well, slept long. Yet woke with this tired feeling. Tired but
nice. It's hard to describe – a kind of joy – I can't stop
smiling – my spirit feels so light. Like that ease you get
after real honest toil, a job well done. But all over now . . .
just relax now. That's how I felt after he'd gone. My visitor,
my special visitor. Chief Leabua Jonathan. The First
Minister of Basutoland. (*Mimics a black voice.*) 'Ow mun,
me is da big chief!' (*Giggles; clears throat.*) Do pardon me.
No, this visit over the weekend really was very important,
it really was. Basutoland was a model for the whole
Bantustan idea. This small little black homeland right in the
middle of South Africa, with its own little parliament, its
own sovereignty, its own identity. So, in effect, this weekend
Chief Leabua Jonathan became the first black statesman . . .
(*Fights giggles.*) . . . to ever visit South African soil. Agh
dear me, the fuss. The way his people had scrubbed and

polished and bathed him. Everybody determined he shouldn't have that, y'know, smell. Shame. Yet things were still slightly wrong, y'know. The aftershave. Even at arm's length. Dear, dear. Poor Betsie, it just made her sneeze. The Noble Savage. (*Giggles.*) 'Yebo, you visit my kraal, now I visit yours.' (*Recovers.*) I think – if I'm permitted to 'psycho-analyse' my behaviour for a moment – I think ever since the elections in March I've been a little light-headed. Winning 126 of the 170 seats – not just a landslide, an earthquake – we have changed the landscape! And no leader this century, not even Smuts, no-one has gained such ascendancy among his people. Yet just consider this. The future will hold many visits from the different Chiefs of the different Bantustans. These Chiefs – they were born here, yet I'll make them aliens. Me – the alien, who came here and made himself Chief. So yes, I looked on this at the weekend and yes allowed myself a liitle smile. (*He reverts to the orator practising his next speech.*) . . . And so my honourable friends, I think this is what the visit of the Prime Minister of Basutoland has symbolised. The Triumph of our Policies. Mr Macmillan's wind of change may well be blowing through this continent, and turning into a veritable hurricane elsewhere – behold the blood in the Congo! – but here it remains just the fairest spring breeze. And so on this fine September day, I think we can afford a smile, a pat on the back, and a sense of . . . a job well done! (*Yawns luxuriously.*) Better get dressed . . .

VERWOERD *exits humming.* BETSIE *comes forward in her nightie.*

BETSIE. He had a restless night. Normally he either sleeps like a log or doesn't sleep at all, isn't even in bed. But there he was next to me, sort of moving and kicking, and making these noises, couldn't tell if it was laughter or tears. I woke with a strange, deep feeling. You know how a bad night can mos' do that to you, hey? Hang over you. So much so that at breakfast I almost said the unthinkable. Don't go to parliament today, lets have a nice drive down to our place at Betty's Bay. Can you imagine his face – ! 'Not go to parliament today? D'you know how important today is!'

(*Smiles affectionately.*) Of course he's going. And me too. This afternoon. To hear him report on the visit from Chief Leba . . . howd'y'sayit? . . . anyhow. (*Sighs.*) Must go splash my face . . . try and wake up properly . . .

BETSIE *exits.* TSAFENDAS *comes forward, fully dressed in his parliamentary messenger uniform.*

TSAFENDAS. Don't know if I slept or not. Can't remember. Was at work at quarter to seven. An hour too early. Filled in time sorting the newspapers. Then just before nine I popped into town. Went to two shops. Bought two knives. Big knives.

LINTWURM *hands him two daggers in their sheaths.*

TSAFENDAS. . . . And then I went back to parliament.

SCHALK. Have to say, none of us even noticed he'd gone. A quiet morning wif the House not sitting till this arvie.

TSAFENDAS. . . . And went into our changing room, the messengers' changing room . . .

He starts fastening the two sheathed knives to a belt. VERWOERD *comes forward, then* BETSIE.

VERWOERD. Spent the morning at a caucus meeting, then in my office. Much to prepare for this afternoon. Not only the Basutoland visit to report. My budget vote is up for discussion. Much to do, much to do.

BETSIE. I spent the morning baking – melktert, his favourite – and doing other preparations for Thursday. Oh, have I mentioned? It's Hendrik's birthday on Thursday. His 65th. We're having a big family supper at home. All them are coming – al die kinders en die kleinkinders – all the family. Lovely.

TSAFENDAS *finishes his belt and locks it in his locker.*

TSAFENDAS. And then I went back to work till lunchtime.

BETSIE. Me and Hendrik were going to have lunch together, but then he rang and said he had meetings right through . . .

VERWOERD. With the Deputy Speaker and the Whip.

BETSIE. I told him not to forget to eat something – just a sandwich or something – he can often forget to eat, y'know.

TSAFENDAS. Can't remember if I had any lunch. Can't remember much about the hour beforehand . . .

SCHALK *positions himself next to a button, wristwatch raised.*

SCHALK. As Senior Messenger I has one of the most important duties of the day. The next action I perform will summon all the members of the House to the Chamber where proceedings will begin at 2.15 prompt, wif the Speaker's procession, the placing of the Mace, the reading of the Prayer. I perform this, my duty, at – precisely – 2.10!

Presses the button. The shrill ringing which we've heard intermittently through the play starts up now – quite low at first – and continues throughout the next section.

TSAFENDAS. I was back in the changing room when I heard the bell go . . .

He takes a deep breath. Unlocks his locker. Takes off his jacket. Straps the belt with knives to his torso. Puts the jacket back on. While this is happening, VERWOERD *and* BUYTENDAG *cross the stage:*

VERWOERD. I heard the bell from my office, and set off for the lobby, my bodyguard Lieutenant-Colonel Buytendag immediately falling in behind.

BUYTENDAG. Armed with police-issue revolver, six rounds, fully loaded, worn in shoulder holster, left side, pack of spare rounds carried in lower jacket pocket, right-side, pair of handcuffs carried in rear trouser pocket, left cheek.

BETSIE *appears, wearing a hat, carrying a handbag.*

BETSIE. I was out on the steps when the bell rang, chatting to some of the other wives. It was a lovely spring day. New season sunshine. Bright but soft y'know.

TSAFENDAS. When I got up to the lobby I almost – straightaway – as I came off the stairs – almost bumped straight into the Prime Minister – !

He and VERWOERD *pass very close.*

TSAFENDAS. . . . Gave me a real fright. A real blood to ice feeling.

VERWOERD. Never even noticed him.

BUYTENDAG (*defensively*). But I did!

VERWOERD. My attention drawn to a party entering the main door . . .

BUYTENDAG. Noticed him, but so what? The messenger boys were everywhere!

VERWOERD. . . . A party of school pupils.

The uniformed PUPILS *arrive.*

PUPIL 1. Matric pupils from the J.J.du Preez Hoerskool in Parow.

PUPIL 2. Here to see the workings of Parliament.

PUPIL 1. Must take notes, write essays afterwards.

PUPIL 2. We're all really very excited.

PUPIL 1. Because the Prime Minister himself will be speaking today!

VERWOERD. . . . And when I saw them I had, y'know, a sense of real pride, and a lovely little feeling went through me – the Future – a little glimpse of the Future.

BETSIE. I came indoors just as he was looking at the children. Such a nice look. That smile of his.

VERWOERD *and* BETSIE *exchange a brief kiss.*

VERWOERD *and* BETSIE (*as one*). See you later, liefling.

BETSIE. The wives have a special bay in the Gallery. So I then went over to the lift.

VERWOERD. And I reached the door of the Chamber.

BUYTENDAG. Where I left him. (*Gulps.*) I had to. I'm not allowed in the Chamber. My position is also up in the Gallery, whereto I now proceeded.

LINTWURM. Shame – his bodyguards didn't have a lodda luck, hey?

VERWOERD goes through the door. TSAFENDAS approaches it.

TSAFENDAS. Once I saw him go in, it started. Like in slow motion. One foot after the other. That's all I can say how it felt.

He goes through the door. Up in the Gallery, BETSIE *appears.*

BETSIE. I settled in my usual seat, and took a moment of quiet contemplation in preparation for the Prayers with which the Speaker would shortly open proceedings.

BUYTENDAG and the PUPILS arrive in the Gallery. Meanwhile downstairs, various key figures are taking their place in the Chamber: JOHN VORSTER, FRANK WARING, DR FISHER, *and* SCHALK. *Murmur and chatter, the bell still ringing.* VERWOERD *enters.*

VERWOERD. I crossed the floor of the House quite briskly, nodding to one or two colleagues . . .

Now TSAFENDAS *enters, reaching under his jacket.*

TSAFENDAS. It was starting, happening, finishing. All at the same time. All very slow. One foot after the other.

WARING. I saw this messenger boy come in . . .

LINTWURM (*naming each MP like a TV commentator*). Frank Waring, Minister for Tourism, Forestry and Sport.

WARING. . . . Just shoving people aside. So I said to Johnnie next to me . . .

LINTWURM. John Vorster, now Minister of Justice and Police.

WARING. . . . Said to ou Johnnie, What's that bloke up to?

VORSTER. And I replied, Probably late for work.

BUYTENDAG (*from the Gallery*). I half-noticed him down there ja, crossing the floor. I thought. isn't that one normally up here – on Press duty? But, y'know, it's not my job to keep track of them all!

The ringing grows louder.

VERWOERD. I reached my seat, I sat down.

TSAFENDAS. He sat down. I couldn't reach the knives.

WARING:. I watched this guy messing with his jacket.

VORSTER. I thought hell he isn't even dressed yet.

TSAFENDAS. I had second thoughts now.

WARING:. I saw him veer over to the Opposition benches.

TSAFENDAS. But only for a second.

WARING:. Then back towards the Prime Minister's desk.

VERWOERD. And that's when I saw him.

TSAFENDAS. He saw me then.

VERWOERD. For the first time.

TSAFENDAS. He'd seen me often before.

VERWOERD. I wondered if I knew this one's name.

TSAFENDAS. Always just looked straight through.

VERWOERD. All these messenger boys.

TSAFENDAS. But he saw me this time.

TSAFENDAS *leans over* VERWOERD*'s desk, struggling to draw a knife.*

VERWOERD. I thought it was a message.

VORSTER. A message – that's what I thought.

WARING. I thought he'd stumbled.

TSAFENDAS. And then I fell . . .

VERWOERD. And then he showed me . . .

TSAFENDAS. I fell towards him.

VERWOERD. . . . . A leather knife, a soft knife . . .

TSAFENDAS. Fell into the thing.

VERWOERD. . . . Was almost comical . . .

TSAFENDAS. Fell to it.

> TSAFENDAS *has finally managed to draw one of the*
> *sheathed daggers. He plucks off the sheath. Stabs*
> VERWOERD *for the first time. In the chest. The blade*
> *goes in deep, to the hilt.* VERWOERD *looks surprised.*

VERWOERD (*slowly*). . . . Heard a voice say 'What a bang' . . .
a boy's voice . . . in Dutch, not Afrikaans . . . then couldn't
think of the Afrikaans for 'What a bang' . . . then thought,
Oh come on this is no time for . . .

> *The ringing increases, drowning him and all other noise.*
> TSAFENDAS *withdraws the knife.* VERWOERD *raises one*
> *arm, but the attack is unstoppable now.* TSAFENDAS *stabs*
> *three more times: to the left side of the neck, to the left lung,*
> *to the right lung.* TSAFENDAS *rocks back.* VERWOERD
> *has a small smile on his face. He remains upright for a*
> *moment. Then sighs. Then slowly slumps forward onto his*
> *desk. The ringing fades to normal volume. Up in the Gallery*
> *people speak quietly, in shock:*

BETSIE. I don't think I saw it happen. Not a hundred percent,
but I think I didn't. Which in the days to come I was to
regard as both a blessing and a sorrow.

PUPIL 1. Was so fast I never even saw the knife.

PUPIL 2. I saw it.

PUPIL 1. OK I saw it too.

PUPIL 2. Saw it but it didn't look real.

PUPILS 1 *and* 2. Our set book's just been 'Julius Caesar'.

BUYTENDAG. Did I see? Did I realise? Uh . . . think it took a
moment.

> *A dazed* BUYTENDAG *exits the Gallery. Downstairs,*
> WARING *rises.*

WARING. I was first off the mark.

LINTWURM. Not only Sports Minister, but former Springbok centre.

WARING (*moving fast*). I vaulted my desk, I crossed the floor, I got the bugger!

He does a spectacular tackle, bringing down TSAFENDAS. *As the others* (VORSTER, FISHER, SCHALK) *rush forward,* WARING *sits up.*

WARING. Can I just show you that again?

OTHERS. Ja, go on, OK, show us Frankie boy . . .

WARING *repeats the action in slow motion – like a match replay – speaking slowly as well:*

WARING. I vault my desk . . . I cross the floor . . . I get the bugger . . .

As WARING *slowly tackles* TSAFENDAS *again, the others cheer like a rubgy crowd, also in slow motion:*

OTHERS. Vrystaaaaat!!

The ringing stops abruptly, and eveything snaps back to reality. The others descend on TSAFENDAS, *punching him savagely. He disappears into their midst. All we hear are blows and heavy breathing: animals on a prey. Up in the Gallery* BETSIE *stands.*

BETSIE. It was the fighting I really noticed first . . . the fighting round his desk. Then I knew something was wrong. Ooh it's a terrible feeling. When you *know* something's wrong.

BETSIE *exits the Gallery. The* PUPILS *hang over the rails, amazed. Down in the Chamber,* BUYTENDAG *reaches the scrum. Someone hands him the bloody dagger. Someone else gives the belt with the second dagger.* BUYTENDAG *sways on his feet.*

LINTWURM. Shame. Poor bastard, hey?

As SCHALK *and* BUYTENDAG *drag* TSAFENDAS *to one side,* VERWOERD *is revealed again, still slumped on his desk.*

VORSTER. Is there a doctor in the House?

FISHER (*bounding forward*). Yes sir.

LINTWURM. Dr. E. Fisher, United Party member for Rosettenville.

FISHER opens VERWOERD's shirt and uses a handkerchief to try and staunch the bleeding. BUYTENDAG and SCHALK start to hustle TSAFENDAS out. He's covered in blood, his own and Verwoerd's.

TSAFENDAS. Where's that poes . . . ? I'll get that pussy poes-fuck . . . !

At the door he almost crashes into BETSIE. They stare at one another. Then TSAFENDAS is taken out and BETSIE enters the Chamber. VORSTER hurries to her.

BETSIE. What have they done to him?

VORSTER. He's been attacked . . . stabbed . . .

BETSIE. Will he live?

VORSTER. We're hoping so. We're praying so.

She crosses to VERWOERD, and strokes his hair, whispering to him.

FISHER. Uhm . . . maybe you should wait outside, Mrs Verwoerd.

VORSTER. Maybe in his office, hey?

BETSIE. I want to stay with him so much.

VORSTER. Ja but I think, Tant Betsie, I think he'd prefer you not to be here.

She hesitates, then stands.

BETSIE. Whatever happens, God does not make mistakes.

She kisses VERWOERD on the forehead, and allows VORSTER to lead her out. As soon as she's gone FISHER hauls VERWOERD onto the ground and starts artificial respiration.

FISHER (*to WARING*). Please – in my office – second drawer in my desk – a phial with coramine on it -

WARING. Coramine.

FISHER. – And a syringe – quick!

WARING *sprints off.* FISHER *starts to massage*
VERWOERD*'s chest. Long silent pause while this happens,
the* PUPILS *gawping from the Gallery.* VORSTER *returns,
stands watching helplessly.* WARING *sprints back with the
phial and syringe.* FISHER *prepares the syringe and injects
it directly into* VERWOERD*'s heart.* SCHALK *and*
BUYTENDAG *return with a stretcher. Everyone helps lift*
VERWOERD *onto it.* BUYTENDAG *puts a blanket on*
VERWOERD, *tucking it under his chin.* FISHER *moves it over
his face. As the men carry out the stretcher,* VERWOERD*'s
left arm slips out, hanging limply. Lights fade on the House
of Assembly as we hear the 4pm radio broadcast:*

VORSTER. . . . With deep regret it is announced that Dr
Verwoerd died after a knife attack this afternoon made by
a temporary parliamentary messenger. The Prime Minister
was rushed to Groote Schuur Hospital but was dead on
arrival. The assassin was immediately arrested, but at the
moment his motives are not known. The police are engaged
in a thorough investigation. In these, for South Africa,
strange times, I want to appeal to everyone to keep calm . . .

As the broadcast continues, we change to . . .

Scene 21

. . . A consulting room. DR GAVRONSKY, *Chief Psychiatrist,
is sitting on a chair, taking notes.* TSAFENDAS *is lying on the
couch. He's very bruised, covered in bandages, his nose in
plaster. He is handcuffed to a* POLICE GUARD *– in fact*
LINTWURM *– who sits alongside, impassive. The radio
broadcast is still half audible from next door.*

TSAFENDAS. What are they saying on the wireless?

GAVRONSKY. That the Prime Minister was stabbed in
Parliament.

TSAFENDAS. That is correct. I remember that happening.
Can't remember much afterwards, but yes I did stab him.
Right through.

GAVRONSKY. And what made you do a thing like that?

TSAFENDAS. I didn't agree with the policies . . .

He suddenly breaks down.

TSAFENDAS. Ai meu Deus . . . por favor, meu Deus . . .

GAVRONSKY. Why are you upset?

TSAFENDAS. Don't know.

GAVRONSKY. Aren't you pleased with what you've done?

TSAFENDAS. Well, I'm a Christian, so how . . . ? But I'm . . . I'm certainly pleased to talk to you. A better class of person. I normally have to mix with . . . (*Mopping his face.*) Mind you, don't know who I'll mix with now. After this business is over. D'you think I might even have to move out of Cape Town? Public opinion, y'know.

GAVRONSKY *stares at him, frowning, then consults his notes.*

GAVRONSKY. Do you ever hear voices? Does God speak to you?

TSAFENDAS. Not personally. Uhm. Only when I'm in bed, fast asleep. Then I feel something that sort of passes me by. There is something . . . spiritual . . . in me. But . . . (*Glances nervously at* GUARD-LINTWURM, *then whispers to* GAVRONSKY.) . . . hard to say if it's always God. Or is it the snake? The Dragon Worm.

GAVRONSKY. I beg your pardon?

TSAFENDAS. Tapeworm I had as a teenager. Grown to giant proportions now, I'm afraid. And very talkative, so be careful . . .

He discreetly indicates GUARD-LINTWURM. GAVRONSKY *is mystified.*

GAVRONSKY. So would you say that this . . . Dragon Worm . . . would you say it drove you to the deed?

TSAFENDAS (*suddenly completely coherent*). No, no, no. Verwoerd. Verwoerd drove me to it. He's an alien. He hasn't

got the people behind him. I see no progress for the African
peoples or the bastard peoples or . . .

GAVRONSKY *looks up from his notes, intrigued.*

TSAFENDAS. . . . This thing has gone too far. Like the sexual
part. The sex laws. Unhallowed unions. The Immorality
Act – telling you who you can't marry – it's immoral. The
only girl who wanted to marry me didn't have the right card.
Can't just keep changing our cards! Dear me. Anyhow . . .

*From the next room the radio is heard playing funereal
music, a slow military march.* TSAFENDAS *listens, then
shakes his head.*

TSAFENDAS. All this is from something I did?

GAVRONSKY. You stabbed the Prime Minister.

TSAFENDAS. That is correct. Right through.

GAVRONSKY. What did you feel when it was happening?

TSAFENDAS (*thinks, then*). Hey presto.

GAVRONSKY *jots a note.* TSAFENDAS *closes his eyes.*
GUARD-LINTWURM *turns to us with a big grin. The
military march grows in volume . . .*

Scene 22

*. . . The day of the state funeral. As the march comes nearer, a
black STREET SWEEPER stops work to watch from the
sidelines. The CAST enter doing a slow-march step, everyone
wearing black hats, black armbands and sunglasses. Draped
in the national flag, VERWOERD's coffin travels on a gun
carriage. Most prominent among the mourners is BETSIE,
determined to be brave. The procession slowly crosses the
stage and exits. As the march fades into the distance, a soaring
African song takes over. The STREET SWEEPER does a
magnificent high-stamping dance of joy – like the Zulu
warriors on the famous Private Eye cover: 'Verwoerd Dead –
A Nation Mourns'.*

Scene 23

. . . The Prime Minister's office. VORSTER *is now in the job, sitting behind* VERWOERD*'s desk, chain-smoking. Opposite him,* DR GAVRONSKY *is reading from notes. The situation mirrors Scene 11.*

GAVRONSKY. . . . Then he said 'He hasn't got the people behind him.'

VORSTER. That's a bloody laugh. When we've just won 126 outta 170 seats. No-one's ever done that before.

GAVRONSKY. I think, Prime Minister, I think he meant . . . the people.

VORSTER. Haah?

GAVRONSKY (*squirming*). The people. All the people who . . . can't vote.

VORSTER *peers at* GAVRONSKY.

VORSTER. Where you from, Dr Gavronsky?

GAVRONSKY. Here. Cape Town.

VORSTER. And your people?

GAVRONSKY (*nervously*). Eastern Europe. Lithuania . . .

He hesitates as VORSTER *jots a note.*

VORSTER. Carry on please.

GAVRONSKY. Ehrm . . . well, he also talked about the Immorality Act. Called it . . . immoral.

VORSTER. Huh! (*Checking a file.*) Ja – even tried to get himself reclassified. Just to go fok some bloody Coloured girl, hey?

GAVRONSKY. Well . . . except of course he *is* Coloured.

VORSTER. Coloured . . . ? (*Confirming in file.*) Jirra! Gonna have to play that one down. When we announce he's Greek, people start attacking Greek shops. We switch to Portuguese, same thing happens. Now if we say Coloured . . . !

GAVRONSKY. Well yes, he complained to me about this very thing . . . (*A weak laugh.*) We're certainly dealing with something of an identity crisis here . . . I think it's fair to say that. (*Checks notes.*) So anyway . . . those were the specifically 'political' references he made during our session.

VORSTER. So whadda your conclusions, Doctor Gavronsky? (*Before* GAVRONSKY *can answer.*) 'Cause I'll tell you mine. The bloke is mad.

GAVRONSKY (*trying a smile*). We've been here before, haven't we? David Pratt, the . . .

VORSTER. Ja. And he was mad too.

GAVRONSKY. Well . . . it was another rather complex case.

VORSTER. Rather simple as I recall it. Either he was mad or we were.

GAVRONSKY *laughs nervously.*

GAVRONSKY. Anyway, regarding Tsafendas, Prime Minister, he told me about this . . . tapeworm.

VORSTER. Tapeworm?

GAVRONSKY. A giant tapeworm. Inside him. Now, just as a precaution we have had his stomach examined and there's no evidence of any infestation by a worm. However, it's only fair to say that if it was the more dangerous species, taenia solium, this can enter the bloodstream and, in extreme cases, affect the brain. I mention this because he reports the worm talking to him. He calls it a snake, the Dragon Worm . . .

VORSTER *rolls his eyes and mutters Afrikaans swearwords.*

GAVRONSKY. Look Prime Minister, from a clinical point of view Tsafendas certainly shows some signs of paranoid schizophrenia . . .

VORSTER. Schizophrenia. OK hang on, hang on. I'm just a simple man Doctor, I haven't got the wisdom of my hallowed predecessor, so pardon me if I go a bit deurmekaar with this talk of snakes and Dragon Worms. But schizophrenia – that just means the bloke's completely fokkin nuts, doesn't it? We need go no further.

GAVRONSKY. Well . . . not quite.

VORSTER *glares at him, jots a note.* GAVRONSKY *mops his brow.*

GAVRONSKY. . . . . The point I wanted to make, Prime Minister, is that alongside this man's symptoms of mental disorder, there is also, one could argue, a fairly clear political motivation. And a personal one. He is, in the end, a Coloured man who has suffered a lifetime of almost unimaginable isolation and dislocation, kicked from one country to another, and it all stems from an initial rejection by *his own family* because of his colour. And this same very displaced, very angry Coloured man then ends up killing the . . . (*He can't say it.*)

VORSTER. Architect of Apartheid.

GAVRONSKY. Just so. However abhorrent and tragic the result, I'm simply saying there is a connection here. There is a clear motive to the man's action. There is some logic. So there is, one could argue, sanity.

Long pause.

VORSTER. Good. Very good. Thank you. For a moment there I was worried you were going to prove him mad. But if he isn't – if he's sane – then good. Then I can hang him.

GAVRONSKY *gulps. At that moment,* MR JUSTICE PIENAAR *enters, a big, broken-nosed Afrikaner.*

VORSTER. Oh good, ja, come in – Doctor Gavronsky this is Mister Justice Pienaar, who's gonna help organise the summary hearing. Doctor Gavronsky was just rushing off.

GAVRONSKY (*hastily collecting papers*). That's right . . . yes . . .

VORSTER. Thank you Doctor Gavronsky. (GAVRONSKY *heads for the door.*) Doctor – thank you.

VORSTER *holds out his hand.* GAVRONSKY *reluctantly surrenders Tsafendas' file. Then exits.*

PIENAAR. Gavronsky. Is he . . . ?

VORSTER. Well, it's not a fokkin Voortrekker name, is it?

PIENAAR *chuckles and sits.* VORSTER *gives him a cigarette.*

PIENAAR. So . . . presumably you want to hang him, Johnnie?

VORSTER. Well actually I wanna remove his balls with my teeth. I wanna skin him alive quite slowly. I wanna cut open, dig out, and unravel his guts before his own amazed eyes. Then I wanna stick hot needles in those eyes. And then I want the best surgeons in the land to patch him up. And then I wanna start all over again. (*A beat.*) Ja, I wanna hang him. And I've just been given permission. (*Thinks.*) I wonder if we could do it publicly. Considering the special circumstances. Or film it definitely.

PIENAAR. Not a good idea.

VORSTER. I was joking. I think.

PIENAAR. No, I mean to hang him at all. Not a good idea.

VORSTER. Haah?

PIENAAR. If you hang him that means he's sane.

VORSTER. Correct – the bloke's sane. The bloke's a fokkin Coloured Commie Griekse Portugees uitlander baster who fokkin killed the greatest fokkin man this country's ever fokkin seen!

PIENAAR. And why did he do that?

VORSTER. 'Cause he hates apartheid, hates the Immorality Act, hates us all.

PIENAAR. Exactly. Which doesn't sound so good. Announced to the world.

Pause.

VORSTER. The bloke is mad.

PIENAAR. Better.

VORSTER. He hears a giant tapeworm, a Dragon Worm talking to him.

PIENAAR. Better still.

VORSTER. There's no political motivation at all.

PIENAAR. Getting even better.

VORSTER. A motiveless attack by a complete fokkin nutcase.

PIENAAR. Perfection. At the hearing we'll say he's unfit to plead or stand trial. We'll say something like: to judge this man would be like judging an animal.

They look at one another.

VORSTER. That was easier than I thought.

PIENAAR. Me too.

VORSTER *produces a bottle of whisky and glasses, and pours out massive shots.* PIENAAR *glances through the Tsafendas file.*

PIENAAR. . . . So his father was fucking one the maids in the house. Good idea. (VORSTER *guffaws.*) I'm serious, man. We must fuck the Coloured white. Our forefathers fucked the kaffir. Thus making the Coloured. Now we must fuck the Coloured. Thus making them white again. End of problem. I'm serious.

VORSTER (*laughing*). I'm scared you are. (*Opens a notepad.*) OK let's work out the details. (*Hesitates.*) Which did we say he was?

PIENAAR. Mad.

VORSTER. Mad. OK, so -?

PIENAAR. An asylum.

VORSTER. Asylum? Bit cushy isn't it? For a fokkin doos like him.

PIENAAR. Well, you can't send him to jail.

VORSTER. Why not?

PIENAAR. Because then he's sane.

VORSTER. I'll send him where I fokkin want – I'm the Prime Minister!

PIENAAR (*cheerfully raising his glass*). Gesondheid!
    (*Dictating as* VORSTER *writes.*) 'Detained for life at

the State President's pleasure.' (*Indicates Tsafendas file.*) What d'you want to do with this?

VORSTER. Don't care – burn it, eat it! (*Writing with increasing fervour.*) And I'm not only gonna send this fokkin doos to a fokkin jail, I'm gonna send him to the fokkinest worst fokkin jail in the whole fokkin land! (*Signs the order.*) When I'm finished with him he's not gonna know his own fokkin face in the mirror . . . !

Scene 24

. . . LINTWURM *and* TSAFENDAS *are standing together, linked by handcuffs, waiting anxiously.*

TSAFENDAS. Always wanted to ask something.

LINTWURM. You ask away buddy.

TSAFENDAS. The meal. When was the meal? When we two actually . . . ?

LINTWURM. At boarding school.

TSAFENDAS. Really? At Middelburg.

LINTWURM. Daar in die ou Transvaal.

TSAFENDAS (*singing quietly*). 'Nou bring my terug . . . '

LINTWURM. 'Na die ou Transvaal . . . '

TOGETHER. 'Daar waar my Saric woon . . . '

TSAFENDAS (*cutting in abruptly*). And this meal was pig – pork?

LINTWURM. Pork chops. Bit bloody round the bone.

TSAFENDAS. And – South African?

LINTWURM. Sorry?

TSAFENDAS. This pork – was it South African?

LINTWURM. Was it South African . . . ! Man, this pork was from a long line of South African pork. This pork went on the Great Trek. This pork fought the Boer War. This pork was so South African it was practically kosher pork.

TSAFENDAS. Funny that.

LINTWURM. Hey?

TSAFENDAS. Everyone's saying, 'The biggest South African crime ever!' Yet think. One party's Dutch. The other's Mozambican-Portuguese-Greek. The only one who's South African is the pork.

LINTWURM. Hey – we've got our guy – arrest the pork!

They smile at one another. Resume waiting.

LINTWURM (*to audience*). They're sending him to Beverly Hills. They call it that, y'know. Because you're gonna see stars. Stars before your eyes. Death Row, Pretoria Maximum Security. They can't hang Demetrios – he's mad – so they've given him life. But. Life on Death Row. In a special cell, right under the gallows. Seven gallows just above him. So he can hear everything that goes on – the before, during, and after. Death Row. Yummy words, hey? Deeaathhhh Ro-ow-oww-wow . . . agh, don't get me started. Basically, he's arriving in hell, folks. Hell on earth . . .

The sound of harsh footsteps approaching.

LINTWURM. They're coming.

TSAFENDAS. Yes. 'm a bit scared.

LINTWURM. Me too, buddy, me too. 'Me – '

TSAFENDAS. ' – And my shadow.'

They nervously dance a few steps of 'Me And My Shadow'.

LINTWURM. But as long as we're together, we -

TSAFENDAS. No.

LINTWURM. What?

TSAFENDAS. I want you to go now.

The footsteps are coming closer.

TSAFENDAS. Please. Quickly.

LINTWURM. You serious?

TSAFENDAS. I'll never get through this with you. All that pussy poes-fuck stuff. They'll kill me. All they'll need is one excuse. And you'll give it to them. I'm going to have to stay very, very quiet now.

LINTWURM. You are serious.

TSAFENDAS. Just go.

LINTWURM *undoes the handcuffs, but doesn't moove. He stares at* TSAFENDAS, *disbelieving.*

TSAFENDAS. Go on. Ai paratamas! Voetsek! Please go.

LINTWURM *starts to leave.* TSAFENDAS *grabs him, hugs him goodbye. They entwine. Both make noises like pining dogs.* LINTWURM *can't let go.* TSAFENDAS *prises them apart, and shoves him away.* LINTWURM *vanishes – just as a group of* WARDERS *arrives. They immediately start hitting* TSAFENDAS *– in a routine way – they've got years and years to do this – and bundle him into a bright, narrow, upright box: a miniature version of a jail cell.* TSAFENDAS *squeezes in, filling it entirely. It's on a pulley system. A shadowy figure positions himself next to the controls. It's* VERWOERD'S GHOST *– as benign and sinister in death as in life. (For the rest of the scene, as* TSAFENDAS *talks to us, the box is repeatedly lifted a foot or so, then dropped abruptly and loudly – jolting him, jolting us – creating the feel of his life on Death Row..)* TSAFENDAS *listens hard; a wave of chatter is coming down the corridor.*

TSAFENDAS (*whispers*). . . . Is this Talking Time? There's a Rule of Silence . . . 23 hours a day. Suppose the others all get it out of their system in this one hour left. Listen. My, my, the jibber-jabber down there. Well, just have to jabber to myself . . . which I've never really minded. And there's always a song in my heart . . .

He sings:

TSAFENDAS. Jeepers creepers
Where d'you get those peepers
Jeepers . . .

He stops, listens. In the distance, a voice panting with terror. Coming closer. Footsteps too. A BLACK PRISONER *passes right in front of him with two* WARDERS. *The footsteps fade. Followed by the sound of winching and creaking.* TSAFENDAS *braces himself. His box lifts and crashes!*

TSAFENDAS. . . . Oooff! Well, well. Still, mustn't complain. Always been my motto. There's bound to be someone worse off than me. Like . . . (*Can't think of an example.*) The warders are a rather crude bunch, I'm afraid . . . a very lowly type of person . . . all Afrikaner fellows, all Verwoerd fanatics . . .

A WARDER *arrives with a plate of food. He puts the plate on the ground, unzips his flies and pisses on the food.* VERWOERD'S GHOST *watches. When the plate is almost overflowing the* WARDER *gives it to* TSAFENDAS. *He doesn't protest or even hesitate – he knows the game – just starts eating. The* WARDER *strolls away.*

TSAFENDAS (*chewing with difficulty*). You get used to it of course . . . bit of a shock at first, of course . . . but then you think, the food in here, maybe it improves the flavour. (*Looks up.*) I think the hardest thing is this light. Never ever turned off. I am getting to miss darkness, I have to admit it. More than even, I don't know, a sea breeze or ice cream in a cone . . .

He listens. Utter silence. He whispers:

TSAFENDAS. Could be in outer space. Could be an Alien. Which they always said I was . . . Undesirable Alien . . .

He sings:

TSAFENDAS. Falling in love again
Never wanted to
What am I to do . . .

He stops, listens. WARDERS *pass with another terrified* BLACK PRISONER. TSAFENDAS *braces himself. His box lifts and crashes!*

TSAFENDAS. . . . And then eventually time passed. Time is amazing y'know when it stops going one-two-three, tick-tock-tick, hard little things, hard working things, time is amazing when it becomes more like . . . dough, water, mud, wind, breath, blood, bowels . . . a chain, lav chain, a worm, tapeworm, a cord, birth cord . . . time is amazing when it starts to deliver, to fold and flop, go backwards, round and round . . . time is amazing when time just passes.

He has grown older. He listens. This time the BLACK PRISONER *who passes is singing N'kosi Sikele in a frightened yet beautiful voice.* TSAFENDAS *braces himself. The box crashes! His voice is starting to assume the odd, broken shout from Scene 1:*

TSAFENDAS. . . . And in this passing of time we were getting . . . d'you know, I think I'm going deaf . . . which might be nice . . . we were getting a different kind of offender . . . very different . . . something was happening outside . . .

The singing of N'kosi Sikele grows, with more and more voices joining in. As if to drown it out, the box lifts and crashes, lifts and crashes – VERWOERD'S GHOST *working the controls robotically – while* TSAFENDAS *is jolted round wildly.*

TSAFENDAS (*singing loudly*). 'Roll out the barrel . . . we'll have a barrel of fun . . . '

His box lifts again. He braces himself. But nothing happens. He strains to listen. The place suddenly seems deserted. There's a slight wind – as though a door is open. He peers round the edge of his box. VERWOERD'S GHOST *is slumped forward, hands off the controls, leaving* TSAFENDAS' *box dangling off the ground. Now* SIPHO – *the black male nurse from Scene 1 – wanders in.*

SIPHO. Demetrios Tsafendas?

TSAFENDAS (*cupping ear*). Wha'?

SIPHO. Give me your hand.

TSAFENDAS. Wha'?

SIPHO *helps the old* TSAFENDAS *onto ground level.*

SIPHO. I'm taking you to Sterkfontein, OK?

TSAFENDAS. Wha'?

SIPHO. Sterkfontein Hospital – just outside Krugersdorp.

TSAFENDAS. Wha's happened?

SIPHO (*shouting into one ear*). It's over.

TSAFENDAS. Wha's over?

SIPHO. Apartheid, man. All over.

TSAFENDAS. Apartheid's over? Bugger me.

> SIPHO *leads* TSAFENDAS *away.* VERWOERD'S GHOST
> *struggles to sit up straight. He's suddenly an ancient,
> delapidated figure – perishing before our eyes – yet raging
> to the end:*

VERWOERD'S GHOST. Apartheid over. Apartheid dead.
South Africa 'reclassified', given a change of ID, and now
known as 'The New South Africa'! I swore it'd never end
except in battle . . . but it's ending with people queueing to
vote. Bantus. Not in their own Bantustans. But here, right
here, in this holy land. It's beyond belief. The weakness of
the men who followed me. It took a foreigner, an uitlander,
to think for them. To carve this piece of earth . . . (*Makes
stabbing gestures.*) . . . here – and here – and here – come,
take this, it's OURS! Sweet Lord, so, so precious. And they
gave it up without even a fight . . . ! (*Pauses in fury,
struggling for breath..*) At least, thank Christ, there's a tiny
group left . . . diehard Boere, bitter-enders . . . ones who
won't surrender. And they have a leader . . . their divine
inspiration . . .

> BETSIE *trudges across the stage, carrying two dusty old
> suitcases – like* TSAFENDAS *in the early scenes. As a few*
> FOLLOWERS *stagger after her, laden with baggage, it's
> almost like a reprieve of* The Ballet of the Suitcases.
> VERWOERD'S GHOST *watches them, his eyes filling.*

VERWOERD'S GHOST. . . . . They're going to buy a small
piece of this good earth, and they'll call it Oranje. And
Oranje will be whites-only. Not even as hewers of wood or
carriers of water will the Bantu ever again be at their side.
No, they will live on their own, proud and pure . . . and they

will beget offspring . . . and these will beget more, and multiply . . . and Oranje, this will become the New South Africa!

The little procession has gone. VERWOERD'S GHOST *writhes and mutters. An* ORDERLY *comes on and helps him into a dressing gown. Other muttering figures shuffle onstage . . . principal characters from the play,* HELEN DANIELS, VORSTER, GAVRONSKY *and others, all wearing the white, coloured-stripe dressing gowns of . . .*

Scene 25

. . . Sterkfontein Hospital, where we first started. The year is 1994. The INMATES *are a listless group, drugged and dozing.* SIPHO *leads in old* TSAFENDAS, *who looks round.*

TSAFENDAS. . . . . 'Andhra moi ennepe Musa, polytropon, Hos mala pola plahti . . . ' So is this it? Finally. Is this home?

SIPHO (*loudly into his ear*). Home sweet home! Even if it smells a little bit, heh?

TSAFENDAS. Tell you what. After 28 years in Beverly Hills. Paradise on earth.

SIPHO (*laughing; helping him into a gown*). OK. And what you most looking forward to? We always like to welcome our friends with a little gift.

TSAFENDAS. Oh . . . darkness. I can't wait to see darkness again . . .

SIPHO *flicks a switch. The stage goes dark, leaving* TSAFENDAS *in silhouette. He wanders round happily, arms raised, fingers playing in the air.*

TSAFENDAS. Oh thank you . . . bless you God for making darkness . . . oh just feel it . . . like silk, like smoke from cooking, like music, like a dream . . .

From the darkness:

A VOICE. . . . A dream . . . of a girl . . . waiting . . . somewhere in Africa . . .

A tight spot reveals it's LINTWURM – *in a dressing gown too. As he speaks,* TSAFENDAS *remains in silhouette, hands lifted, touching the darkness.*

LINTWURM. . . . Well, he never did get the girl, folks. Never did get much of anything, poor old doos, not even an answer to that simplest of all questions – 'Who am I?' OK well – who was he, what was he? Greek, Mozambican, South African? A tramp, a traveller, a messenger? Was he white, was he black? He really couldn't say, nobody could. Not till after the deed, the ass-as-sin-nation, and then he just became the Man Who Killed The Pig. But the question of his ID never died, not even when he did, here in this hospital in '99. None of his family came to the funeral, 'course not, but a whole load of media folk rolled up, and a lotta cops too, along with their sniffer dogs – who all started to howl when a big wreath of white lillies was carried into the service . . .

He pauses, listening to the dogs – as the wreath is put down in his spot. He bends, looks at the message, chuckles.

LINTWURM. . . . Ooh Jesus – a fan. Probably 'political.' Ja. Listen . . . (*Reads.*) 'Dimitri Tsafendas, 1918-1999 . . . Displaced Person . . . Sailor . . . Christian . . . Communist . . . Liberation Fighter . . . Political Prisoner . . . Hero.'

LINTWURM *winks, grins, and is about to sign off, when* TSAFENDAS *suddenly turns.*

TSAFENDAS. . . . And what about Professor of English?!

Lights fade. End of play.